FROM SCAPEGOATS TO LAMBS

How God's Word Speaks to George Floyd's Murder

CHARLES L. BROWN JR.

authorHOUSE®

AuthorHouse™
1663 Liberty Drive
Bloomington, IN 47403
www.authorhouse.com
Phone: 833-262-8899

Published by AuthorHouse 07/07/2021

ISBN: 978-1-6655-2929-7 (sc)
ISBN: 978-1-6655-2930-3 (hc)
ISBN: 978-1-6655-2931-0 (e)

Library of Congress Control Number: 2021912005

Print information available on the last page.

Cover design by Angel Bolques Jr.

This book is printed on acid-free paper.

To Charles Lee Brown Sr. & Mary Louise Brown,
Because of you Mom & Dad, Michael and I have big shoes to fill;
I pray this work reflects you both empowering us to fill them.

He was despised and rejected by others;
a man of suffering and acquainted with infirmity;
and as one from whom others hide their faces he was despised,
and we held him of no account.

Isaiah 53:3 (New Revised Standard Version)

"But Jesus said to them, "Have you come out with swords and clubs,
as though I were a criminal, to capture Me?"

Mark 14:48 (Holman Christian Standard Bible Version)

"When the Roman officer overseeing the
execution saw what had happened,
he worshiped God and said, "Surely this man was innocent."

Luke 23:47 (New Living Translation)

CONTENTS

ACKNOWLEDGMENTS

First and foremost, I thank God for giving me this divine assignment. Two women, Dr. Clarice Martin, former New Testament professor at Princeton Theological Seminary, and my mother, Mary Louise Brown, author of *Integration: A Doorway to Success*, gave me the exact same challenge almost 30 years apart: "you should write a book." I responded to Dr. Martin, saying that only the black bourgeois read books; the masses love to watch television, and I told my mom that when God gives me a book to write, I would do it. I look back on those exchanges and now see how easily the male disciples in the gospels failed to believe the account from the women on Resurrection Sunday that Jesus is risen, yet the women turned out to be right all along. I could never repay you, Lord, for birthing in me this task to complete, which you prophesied in women long before I could ever imagine this publication.

To my dad, Charles Lee Brown Sr., my brother Michael, my sister-in-law Katina, and my extended family who have been a tremendous source of encouragement; your support has made the difference and I appreciate it. To the Rev. Deborah Finley-Jackson, I thank you not only for assisting me in accessing critical references for this work, but more importantly because your tenacity in earning your PhD this year inspired me. To Deborah Ly and Pam Shaw, thank you for being steadfast encouragers, consistently nudging me to push toward completion. I want to thank a person who shall remain anonymous, and yet I publicly acknowledge that through them my eyes were opened to see how the world of book publishing has dramatically changed since my days in seminary. Thank you to the African Methodist Episcopal Church for training me to be the servant leader I am. To the clergy and congregations of Greater Mt. Nebo A.M.E. Church in Bowie, MD, Campbell A.M. E. Church in Washington, DC, St. Stephens

A.M.E. Church in Elkridge, MD, Bridge St. A.M.E. Church in Brooklyn, NY, St. James A.M.E. Church in Hightstown, NJ, and my home church, Bethel A.M.E. Church in Baltimore, MD. In September of this year, I will commemorate thirty-five years in ministry, and I am grateful that each of these branches of Zion loved unconditionally, challenged and molded me, and groomed me into the leader I am today. I want to thank my "latest" church family, Family of Faith African Methodist Episcopal Church in St. Thomas, USVI. The weekly sacred ritual of mining scripture and connecting the dots to create messages that speak to our unique context has helped me hone a craft that is an essential element of this publication. Thank you to the people of the US Virgin Islands, and especially former Senator Clarence Payne, who has been a friend and confidant in this chapter of my life and also served as a cheerleader on this project. Our work as co-founders of the Virgin Islands Alliance for Consumer Justice influences how I envision the power and purpose of grassroots advocacy working with political leaders to impact lives. It is significant that God gave me the word "scapegoat" in St. Thomas, and being in this unique locale shaped how I understood what God was saying, and how I received God's call for this mission. Special thanks to the Rev. Dr. Mikie Roberts, for being a brother from another mother, and giving me space just to be Charles. Every minister needs at least one person who they can engage in authentic fellowship, liberated from the titles we acquire and just be themselves.

Finally, I need to thank the intellectual giants and spiritual leaders who have inspired me along my journey, beginning with my father-in-ministry, Bishop John R. Bryant, Bishop E. Anne Henning Byfield, Dr. Cornel West, Dr. Michael Eric Dyson, Dr. Jeremiah Wright, Dr. Obery Hendricks (who helped me see and appreciate what he has coined guerrilla exegesis at Princeton Theological Seminary), Dr. Charles E. Lewis, Jr., Congressman Danny K. Davis, Dr. Rodney Sadler and Dr. Tyrone Cass Ross. In their own ways, these heavyweights pushed my critical thinking skills to the brink, and my exposure to them has significantly affected me for the better.

To my super-editor, Ms. Johanna Leigh, who took one look at my introduction and made me feel like this work would change the world! Beyond merely proofreading my manuscript, she believed in the purpose of the work, and the finished product shows not just attention to detail but careful revisions that reflect a passion to make a difference. A huge thank you to Kelly, and the whole team at AuthorHouse Books who worked expeditiously on this project, and for shepherding me through the tedious process of book publishing. I am grateful for your invaluable assistance.

INTRODUCTION

One boring afternoon as a teenager, I was channel surfing and stumbled upon a wildlife documentary that stopped me in my tracks. A herd of zebras was congregating adjacent to a brush harbor when a lion inadvertently detected them from a distance and slowly made its way toward the zebras in stealth mode. Suddenly the lion leaped into the foreground causing one baby zebra to panic and in a matter of seconds, the lion tracked the confused zebra and initially snared the young mammal with the claws in its paws. Almost immediately, as if driven by nature, the lion pounced on the zebra, and just when I thought it would brutally maul the zebra, killing it instantly, the lion opened its mouth extremely wide, and lunged for the zebra's neck, using its four long canines as a vice grip, completely encompassing the zebra's neck, and then waited patiently for the life to slowly seep out of the young mammal. The lion was neither in a frenzy of rage, nor out of control; it was content allowing the zebra to attempt to reposition itself so it could breathe, if not free itself, but the lion had mastered its hunting technique, effectively putting a chokehold on the zebra to precisely rob it of the ability to breathe.

The other zebras watched in horror from a safe distance away—both terrified and mesmerized by the torture of one of their own. They snorted and brayed at the lion as if to curse at it for killing in cold blood, but the lion simply looked at them nonchalantly and casually while its canines suffocated its victim. Slowly but surely the zebra's movements lessened and finally the young mammal went limp, a victim of a calculating predator that was addicted to the thrill of striking terror and killing its prey deliberately and methodically.

Fast forward many decades later to May 25, 2020, and the recording of former Minneapolis police officer Derek Chauvin's behavior as he confronted George Floyd revealed that it is quite possible, Chauvin may have watched some of the same wildlife documentaries on lions hunting their prey in his lifetime. What the videos show is a predator neither out of control, nor accidentally killing George Floyd, but one who had become well-acquainted with modes of torturing and dehumanization. His facial expressions gave away that this methodology of policing was not new for him; and indeed, PBS NewsHour did some digging, and their investigators uncovered firsthand accounts from the victims in six cases where the Attorney General had concluded that Derek Chauvin had used excessive force. Just as the lion uses its power to inflict terror in order to legitimize its supremacy in the animal kingdom, on May 25, 2020, we saw a man comfortable weaponizing his badge, his gun, and his blue uniform to terrorize a community. This is simply how Derek Chauvin operated.

However, due to circumstances beyond his control, the trial lay bare for all to see, the damage to the blue wall of solidarity that normally would be able to withstand any pressure that would present itself on the rare occasion that an officer was forced to defend their actions in court. For some reason, this time the blue wall collectively threw one of its own under the bus, as multiple members of the law enforcement from the Minneapolis Police Department stated in no uncertain terms that using a knee-on-the-neck chokehold for nine minutes and twenty-nine seconds was not a part of any sanctioned police training. I watched horrified as multiple recorded videos showed how those officers treated George Floyd's body like it was an animal, and it took me all the way back to my teenage years watching documentaries of lions hunting and asphyxiating their prey.

For many of us, this brutal execution was a replay of a bad recording spun over and over. Emmett Till, Medgar Evers, James Chaney, Fred Hampton, Robert Hoyt, Amadou Diallo, Trayvon Martin, Michael Brown, Sylville Smith, Sandra Bland, Philando Castile, and the list goes on. Let's not forget the lynchings of the 19th and 20th centuries, the Rosewood massacre; the Tulsa, Oklahoma massacre; the Orangeburg massacre, the Wilmington, DE race riot, and so many others where law enforcement often comingled with members of the community to use violence on black and brown bodies. Different names, familiar narratives. And yet at the same time, I think that a growing segment of the population has sensed that something different occurred in this killing, separating this moment in time from other killings.

When I saw the video of George Floyd's murder, I asked God to show me in a profound way what is going on here. Help us understand this sickening phenomenon . . . not just this killing, but this runaway train of state-sanctioned senseless violence that privileges law enforcement to terrorize with impunity as long as they can say they feel threatened—whether a threat exists or not. How does your Holy Word Jehovah, written thousands of years ago, enlighten and empower us in this moment? What are the dynamics at play which have brought us to this moment and keep us stuck in this space of reoccurring police brutality combined with no accountability? As men and women of faith, how can we get more folks to see that all lives can't matter until *black lives matter*? Whether or not the agenda of white supremacy is ever permanently nullified or not, what are the strategies that can neutralize if not overturn evil's obsession with violating black and brown bodies?

In asking these questions from God, like Jacob wrestling with the angel and refusing to let go until the angel blessed him, God blessed me with one word: scapegoat. I took that one word and crafted a sermon, and by the end of the sermon, God had given me the template for this publication. This then is the goal of *From Scapegoats to Lambs: How God's Word Speaks to George Floyd's Murder*. God may allow all manner of evil to persist, but simultaneously, God delights in equipping men and women of faith with the tools to triumph over evil even in death.

Chapter One teases out the juxtaposition of how the death of George Floyd and its aftermath serve as flashpoints that have ushered in a distinct *Kairos* moment, catalyzing a movement that still persists a year later, and that his death and the aftermath are inextricably tied to the legacies of police brutality in America specifically, and the legacy of the dehumanization of black and brown bodies systemically. In the weeks and months that followed this murder, the needle has moved, the veil has been lifted to some degree, the paradigm has shifted, and the landscape has changed. For a variety of reasons, the death of George Floyd has become an unmistakable fault line in the annals of history such that I believe scholars will look back one day and compare and contrast how we looked at police brutality before George Floyd and now after George Floyd. At the same time, by tying George Floyd's death to the larger legacy of dehumanization of black and brown bodies, the narrative is driven home that what happened is much bigger than one man and one murder, and why the power of his one death is immeasurable when it is connected to a past with roots that run centuries deep.

Chapter Two details the theological history and significance of scapegoating by looking into the significance of the Jewish festival called Yom Kipper, mining through the exegetical insights of Leviticus 16, and tracking how some scholars value its connections to ancient Near Eastern narratives outside the Bible, while others have found the underpinning of scapegoating in the OT narrative of Joseph's brothers kidnapping and selling him as a slave in Genesis 37:12-36. In this way, we begin to examine the roots of communal scapegoating in the Bible to set the foundation for seeing whether those same dynamics are at play today.

Chapter Three looks at the violent scapegoating of a Suffering Servant, by doing a deep dive into the nature of interpreting Isaiah 53 from the realization of oppression heaped upon an individual by a community and how such realization transforms who the facilitators of oppression are and how the world sees the oppressed. It is in the Suffering Servant motif that the notion of redemptive suffering finds resonance in the African American experience of marginalization and dehumanization by the other yet finding validation and empowerment through the suffering in a way that exposes the wickedness of the perpetrators of violence and makes known the sovereignty of the Almighty to redeem those deemed unworthy.

Chapter Four looks at the ministry of Jesus as told in the four gospels and chronicles how from just after His birth, until His death, Jesus is compelled to address the scapegoat narrative. I compare how the purpose, and persona of each of the four gospels' writings influence how they portray the way Jesus deals with scapegoating, and in so doing, gives us strategies and examples for how we can address scapegoating today.

Chapter Five attempts to connect the dots between the scapegoating dynamics between Joseph and his brothers, Leviticus 16, Isaiah 53, and scapegoating in the gospels with the vicious communal scapegoating in the form of George Floyd's murder. I contend that in death George Floyd triumphed over evil as his death became a community sacrifice, transforming him from a defeated scapegoat to a victorious lamb.

Chapter Six is a tribute to the father of the Scapegoat Mechanism, Rene Girard. His two works largely dedicated to the subject, *The Scapegoat* and *Violence and the Sacred* are briefly analyzed and then I attempt to use my customized, hood hermeneutic (i.e. street interpretive framing) to both support and challenge his ethos.

Chapter Seven is the flushing out of—now that we know how scripture speaks to our current context in very profound ways—what do we do about it? Will communal recognition, shaming, and neutralization of oppressive scapegoating help us advance as a human race? This final chapter teases out a Lamb motif that takes us from reactionary protest to strategic, empowering protest that will position us to open more eyes and pull down strongholds. Is the persistence of racism in the form of white supremacy something that white folks alone must address, or if not, what can we do to access power as victims of violent scapegoating, to move us toward a more sacred definition of community?

This book is for people looking for a moral compass to help make sense out of the chaos, to illuminate hidden truths, and to guide them through these turbulent times as the world dares to confront in a significant way, the dehumanization of black and brown bodies head-on. As my cousin, Milton Taylor told me, "The planet is reeling," as so many are now (finally) realizing the severity of racism in our global community, finally beginning to assess the depth of its stranglehold in our culture, our way of life. *From Scapegoats to Lambs* is a book that attempts to understand the addiction of violating marginalized communities and provide compelling explanations for our plight specifically as it relates to state-sponsored violence by law enforcement. As a preacher, public policy advisor and now as church planter/pastor, I have always been driven to uncover how divine revelation can speak to current circumstances in profound ways, that we may press our way forward grounded in Holy Scripture. My goal is for this book to show how the Bible sheds valuable light on the dynamics behind the legacy of dehumanizing black and brown people, especially as it relates to police brutality. At the same time, it is a clarion call for black and brown people to move beyond calling out racism, to positioning ourselves to be agents of transformation, that God would show us how to be change agents, used by God to turn evil's agenda on its head and convert chaos into God's global community.

In February 1991, after some reflection, Lerone Bennett Jr. of Ebony Magazine wrote: "The voices of the past speak to us personally, calling us by name, asking us what have we done, and what we are prepared to do to ensure that the slaves, activists, and martyrs, did not dream and die in vain? . . . Speaking to us, warning us, telling us, how they got over and what we must do to overcome . . . We must relate these images to the challenges and opportunities of our own lives, or we shall learn nothing, and remember nothing."

CHAPTER 1

The More Things Change, the More They Stay the Same

May 25, 2020 was a watershed moment in the fight for social justice as it relates to the legacy of police brutality against black and brown people. That was the day Derek Chauvin, with the assistance of three other police officers, murdered George Floyd. I don't use the word murder lightly or as a weapon, as I believe you can't call what happened anything short of that when a man sworn to serve and protect put his knee on someone's neck for over nine minutes until life left his body. Even as a black man, I can't begin to contemplate what it must feel like to be dehumanized in such a callous manner, but I do understand that I can be perceived to be a threat at any moment regardless of my words or actions. On any given day, a member of a police department (or individuals feeling emboldened to personify law enforcement), could choose to justify the use of excessive force and many in society will jump to the conclusion that I had to be doing something criminal. That it is acceptable for cops to feel threatened by someone unarmed when they are black. That officers who fail to utilize de-escalation tactics they would otherwise use on white people should nevertheless get the benefit of the doubt.

May 25th was a gruesome day, but thank God, it was also a day of metamorphosis. It was a day when cops killing another unarmed black man would solicit an unprecedented outcry from the world. Why did the murder of George Floyd become a watershed moment in time? First and foremost, when I say that this is a "moment in time," what I mean is that this is a most opportune moment, or the right time, both phrases of which are defining characteristics of a Greek word known as *Kairos*. In archery, *Kairos* refers to an opening or 'opportunity' or more precisely, a long tunnel-like aperture through which the archer's arrow must pass. Successful passage of a *Kairos* moment requires, therefore, that the archer's arrow be fired not only accurately but with enough power for penetration. The second meaning of *Kairos* traces to the art of weaving. There is 'the critical time' when the weaver must draw the yarn through a gap that momentarily opens in the warp of the cloth being woven. "Putting the two meanings together, one might understand *Kairos* to refer to a passing instant when an opening appears which must be driven through with force if success is to be achieved." As preachers, we believe that God governs time continually, but every now and again, God chooses to break into time and alter reality. Those nine minutes and twenty-nine seconds resulting in Derek Chauvin asphyxiating George Floyd changed reality; and unbeknownst to him, transformation was fulfilled. The first part of this chapter is about examining what was groundbreaking about the murder of George Floyd and why; the second part of this chapter is about why, despite all the uniqueness of the moment, the death of an unarmed black man by police officers is nothing new to American discourse, not at all! The killing of unarmed black men and women in the United States is as American as apple pie.

While George Floyd's murder is not the only murder of an unarmed black man that was not justified, the feelings evoked from watching his killing left most people perceiving that of all the cases of excessive force, this one clearly was unjustified. The fact that the execution was recorded from multiple perspectives in broad daylight telling the same unified narrative helped drive that point home. That Derek Chauvin had his knee on George Floyd's neck for at least nine minutes and twenty-nine seconds also contributed to the same conclusion. The shock of seeing the callous expression on Derek Chauvin's face as he murdered George Floyd supported the notion. The reality that it is nearly impossible to perceive someone being a threat when they are pinned to the ground face down, with their hands handcuffed behind their back, also lends itself to the same conclusion. All of these factors coalesced to compel more eyes to see the fact of racism being alive and well, that white supremacy is real, and left unchecked—it threatens to tear down our "glorious" democracy that has been violently scapegoating black folks since its founding. In one pregnant moment in time, the hypocrisy of America's moral integrity was exposed for the world to see. Even Republicans who had never conceptualized the injustice of police brutality, admitted full stop that the killing was indefensible. The few Candace Owens of the world, who desperately tried to make criminality stick, failed to make any justification resonate. With regard to many other police killings, there often was a controversial action that opened the door for characterizing someone as a threat. Not so this time. This concrete lynching was too cut and dry. George Floyd was accused of passing a fake $20 bill that day, but in no way did that allegation or anything he did during his encounter with police that day justify him being killed. This wasn't a frenzied, reactionary response to an escalation of tension that suddenly got out of control. It was methodical and again, the expression on former police officer Derek Chauvin's face indicated that his actions were not accidental, if not premeditated.

These factors triggered a comprehensive, visceral outcry from the local, national, and global community demanding for the police officers to be held accountable. The universal backlash of George Floyd's murder by the police was unparalleled. This singular murder united all 50 states and America's territories with many nations around the world.

Here in America, protests were held in the usual large cities and municipalities from the East Coast to the West Coast, but what made this killing unique was that sizable protests broke out in "smaller cities and regions including Wilmington, North Carolina; New Bern, North Carolina; Cedar City, Utah; Bend, Oregon; Crested Butte, Colorado; Auburn, Alabama; Odessa, Texas; Chagrin Falls, Ohio; Chehalis, Washington; Bridgehampton, New York; Havre, Montana; Grand Forks, North Dakota; Wellsville, New York; and Grand Island, Nebraska. Trump won in all those municipalities in 2016, and they are represented in Congress by Republicans. In fact, precedent was recognized two weeks after George Floyd's murder, 'This was really the first protest that has taken place in our city that I can remember, and a lot of our residents were concerned that what has happened in so many other cities would happen in Loganville, (Georgia),' Ray Martinez, a Republican (mayor), told CNBC."

In Great Britain, thousands gathered to join a Black Lives Matter march at Trafalgar Square in London on Sunday, May 31, less than a week after the murder of George Floyd. On that same day in Germany, rallies were held against racism in front of the Brandenburg Gate in Berlin. In the days and weeks following the killing, rallies also took place in Kenya, Ghana, South Africa, Niger, and Senegal. The Chadian Chairperson of the African Union Commission, Moussa Faki Mahamat, was very quick to react to George Floyd's death, calling it a "murder" as early as May 29. In a statement, he said he "strongly condemns the murder of George Floyd that occurred in the United States at the hands of law enforcement officers." "Recalling the historic Organisation of Africa Unity (OAU) Resolution on Racial Discrimination in the United States of America made by African Heads of State and Government, at the OAU's First Assembly Meeting held in Cairo, Egypt from 17 to 24 July 1964, the Chairperson of the African Union Commission firmly reaffirms and reiterates the African Union's rejection of the continuing discriminatory practices against Black citizens of the United States of America," the statement continued.

Protests were also sparked in France, Denmark, Italy, Syria, Mexico, Brazil, New Zealand, Canada, Poland, Australia and Ireland. "People in Ireland are seeing what's happening and we are just as angry and frustrated," marcher Anna Herevin told CNN. "The protest was a show of solidarity with our friends in the US but also a united stand against endemic racism, which is a global threat. In terms of solidarity protests with a movement in another country, this was the biggest I've seen," she said.

The solidarity enjoyed across state and country boundaries united around the cry to arrest the police officers responsible for George Floyd's death. The immediate pressure undoubtedly contributed to Hennepin County Attorney Mike Freeman arresting Derek Chauvin the same week of the murder. "This is by far the fastest we've ever charged a police officer," he stated.

One would think that throughout the legacy of police brutality in America, the swift arrest of police officers would not be unusual. However, according to the 1989 Supreme Court case Graham versus Conner, the legal "reasonableness" standard must take into account what was going through the mind of the cop in the few seconds when he chose to use force and whether their decision was "reasonable" (as defined by what cops in a similar situation would think) under the circumstances at that time, not with the benefit of hindsight.

Not only was Derek Chauvin's arrest and charge undoubtedly influenced by tremendous public pressure, but the other three officers who pinned down George Floyd's legs were eventually charged as well. Hennepin County Judge Peter Cahill also ruled the ex-cops will be tried at the same time in the county on March 8 for charges stemming from a death that was caught on video and became part of a rallying cry for police brutality around the country. He ruled that holding a single proceeding for the four officers would ensure that jurors understand "all of the evidence and the complete picture of Floyd's death . . . And it would allow this community, this State, and the nation to absorb the verdicts for the four Defendants at once," Cahill wrote in his ruling.

Be that as it may, Derek Chauvin was ultimately allowed to stand trial by himself and the other officers will have their day in court eventually. The unprecedented outcry of the masses was bolstered by celebrities and other national figures using their platforms to protest and give monetary support to George Floyd's family, the protestors arrested, and the BLM movement overall. The BLM movement had effectively been launched during the murder of Michael Brown in Ferguson, Missouri in 2014, but George Floyd's murder compelled the national fermentation of two different political campaigns; "Defund the Police," a push to reallocate specific resources from police departments to other essential social services of government. "Different from abolishing and starting anew, defunding police highlights fiscal responsibility, advocates for a market-driven approach to taxpayer money and has some potential benefits that will reduce police violence and crime." The other police reform initiative that gained national significance during the aftermath of George Floyd's murder is abolishing qualified immunity. The doctrine of qualified immunity protects government officials from liability for civil damages insofar as their conduct does not violate clearly established statutory or constitutional rights that a reasonable person would have known. (63C American Jurisprudence, Second Edition, Public Officers and Employees, August 2011.)

Congress responded to these issues by introducing multiple legislation, one aimed directly at qualified immunity (Ending Qualified Immunity Act), and the other addressing police reform holistically to include defunding the police and abolishing qualified immunity (George Floyd Justice in Policing Act of 2020). When introducing the legislation, Representative Justin Amash, a Libertarian from Michigan stated, "The brutal killing of George Floyd by Minneapolis police is merely the latest in a long line of incidents of egregious police misconduct. This pattern continues because police are legally, politically, and culturally insulated from consequences for violating the rights of the people whom they have sworn to serve. That must change so that these incidents of brutality stop happening." The bill's diverse sponsorship by members of the Libertarian, Republican, and Democratic parties makes it the first bill to have tripartisan support in Congress.

On the other hand, the George Floyd Justice in Policing Act would: 1) establish a national standard for the operation of police departments; 2) mandate data collection on police encounters; 3) reprogram existing funds to invest in transformative community-based policing programs; and 4) streamline federal law to prosecute excessive force and establish independent prosecutors for police investigations. On March 3, 2021, the House passed the George Floyd Justice in Policing Act largely along party lines, although I can't ignore that one Republican lawmaker from Texas, was sabotaged by three other Republican members, who tried to change his vote in favor of the bill. Rep. Lance Gooden (R-TX) cast a vote in support of the legislation, but his state Republican colleagues freaked out and each of them attempted to change the vote of Rep. Lance Gooden by signing Gooden's name to the red tally card through the Tally Clerk, a clear violation of House rules. The justification Republicans hide behind to advocate for voter suppression policies is fear of voter fraud, and yet three Republican lawmakers had no problem committing voter fraud on the House floor, in a failed attempt to prevent one Republican from voting for the George Floyd Justice in Policing bill.

In June of 2020, Mississippi began working on legislation aimed at changing the state's flag, which had carried the Confederate battle emblem on it for over 126 years. On Tuesday, November 3, 2020, voters in Mississippi approved a new flag, "The New Magnolia," featuring a magnolia flower. With Mississippi being the last state in the US to have a flag that featured the Confederate battle emblem, #BlackLivesMatter protests that followed the death of George Floyd compelled the state to change its flag.

Trump responded to the aftermath of George Floyd's murder by signing an executive order outlining White House priorities for police reform, which included the creation of a national police misconduct database. The order also created new guidelines for use of force and de-escalation and proposed an increased role for social workers and mental health professionals in responding to a variety of issues. Noticeably absent was any reform to limit qualified immunity for police officers or a ban on chokeholds.

Speaking of banning chokeholds, the Minneapolis city council forced the police department to ban chokeholds and neck restraints. The Louisville police department under pressure—after the death of Breonna Taylor that happened just a few short months before George Floyd—ceased utilizing unannounced police raids, known as "no-knock warrants."

By the end of the year, several metropolitan areas, responding to the #BlackLivesMatter protests in their jurisdictions over the killing of George Floyd over the summer, moved to "Defund the Police." Minneapolis, New York City, Cook County, Illinois and Portland, Oregon all redirected funds away from police departments to other social and mental health services with the hope to see professionals who are qualified to de-escalate distinctive scenarios deployed so that black and brown unarmed individuals can live after an encounter with police officers.

All of this new activity that bubbled up begs the question why? After Rodney King's deadly assault in LA in 1991, after Trayvon Martin was murdered in Sanford, Florida in 2012, and after Mike Brown was gunned down in Ferguson, Missouri in 2014, we experienced movements that laid the foundation for the summer of 2020, but with all due respect to those social justice efforts, they just cannot compare to the momentum and leverage generated by George Floyd's murder. On the one hand, it may not be fair to compare and contrast these *Kairos* moments in history, but on the other hand, I am convinced that fruitful analysis of these movements, and understanding the factors that shaped them can provide information to push the needle forward. The monikers "enough is enough" and "I'm sick and tired of getting sick and tired" apply when we look at those sworn to protect and serve literally getting away with murder. We've already mentioned the length of time Derek Chauvin's knee was pressed on George Floyd's neck and the fact that George Floyd was pinned down and completely immobilized, face down and handcuffed behind his back, stripping the officers of the notion that they were required to make any split-second decision reacting to an imminent threat. It all being caught on video and the expression on Derek Chauvin's face spoke volumes. To those elements, I agree with others that additional factors played a part as to why this murder solicited an unprecedented global response. George Floyd's murder was tied to the murders of Ahmaud Arbery and Breonna Taylor. Three murders in less than 65 days. Different scenarios, but the same results undeniably transmitting the same message; that black people are often treated differently by law enforcement than white people. Jogging down the street or being handcuffed behind your back as you are pinned to the ground do not justify the use of deadly force. The close proximity of these three murders—along with a white woman weaponizing her privilege to call the police, falsely stating that a black man threatened her in Central Park on the very same day George Floyd was murdered in Minneapolis—all combined to light a fuse that exploded into a movement that struggles to stay relevant but gets triggered every time police use excessive force against black and brown bodies.

Another factor that contributed to the aftermath of George Floyd's murder being so intense was the fact that the global pandemic gave millions of unemployed and/or shuttered Americans who were forced to remain indoors because of government restrictions, unfettered, instantaneous access to social media, which broadcasted the slow agonizing lynching of George Floyd for everyone to see. More Americans in their households and on social media or video conferencing in 2020 than ever before, instead of at work, meant more eyes seeing this execution with their own eyes, and that contributed to the scope of protests springing up all over the country.

Internationally, the blatant use of excessive force wielded upon George Floyd resonated with African nations that have historically had chronic issues with police violence. In South Africa, Economic Freedom Fighters (EFF) protesting at the US Embassy in Pretoria, paid tribute to Floyd by taking a knee and observing 9 minutes and 29 seconds of silence—the time it took for him to die under the knee of a police officer. "Enough with police brutality on our black bodies," EFF leader Julius Malema told the crowd, standing next to the wife of a man recently killed by the South African Army enforcing the COVID-19 lockdown. "In Kenya, portraits of George Floyd plastered the walls of Nairobi. And on the same day as in South Africa, about 200 people demonstrated against police violence in the Mathare slum in the capital. Police violence has claimed at least 15 lives in Kenya since a curfew was imposed to prevent the spread of COVID-19." This willingness to globally connect the dots of police violence upon black bodies is what makes the *Kairos* moment of George Floyd's death and its aftermath distinctive.

Another factor that contributed to why this death was different was having the ability to witness on social media and other news outlets, the heavy-handed, militaristic approach by law enforcement against peaceful protestors and media. Seeing a black CNN reporter, Omar Jimenez, get handcuffed live on air for merely reporting on the protests in Minneapolis, was traumatic to watch. Witnessing police tear-gas and violently manhandle protestors to clear a path for then-President Trump to make his way to St. John Episcopal Church for a photo-op became an accelerant for more protestors to join the movement from sectors and demographics who had resisted protesting for previous killings.

Trump's penchant for violent rhetoric incited unprecedented reactions that translated into more and more people injecting themselves into the cause. One of Trump's famous tweets on the protests was, "These THUGS are dishonoring the memory of George Floyd," he wrote, "and I won't let that happen. Just spoke to Governor Tim Walz and told him that the military is with him all the way. Any difficulty and we will assume control but, when the looting starts, the shooting starts. Thank you!" As if it was his sacred, holy duty as commander-in-chief to violently purge the community of mostly peaceful protestors who dared to cross the line. Yet when the violent extremists strategically planned an insurrection, killed one police officer, defecated, vandalized, looted, and pillaged the Capitol building on January 6, his silence during the first few hours was deafening. Serial scapegoaters have no shame grasping any narrative, no matter how flimsy, that justifies their dysfunction. Fortunately, serial scapegoaters often miscalculate and fail to anticipate that their actions towards those they scapegoat sometimes backfire and create a larger-than-life moment of which they have little or no control. When Trump made his racist statement about the shooting starting when the looting starts, he had no clue how incendiary his comments would be; that his words would be a rallying cry for more people to protest, instead of them fearing the threat of violence. When Derek Chauvin pressed his knee on George Floyd's neck, he was hoping it would end just as other countless killings of unarmed black Americans ended. If he knew that his actions were going to inflict stiff consequences, would he have done the same thing? The brutality of his attack indicates his mindset entering an alternate reality where he believed his actions were totally appropriate. His facial expression showed a level of calm while doing something so violently cruel and in so doing, it unwittingly contributed to the transfer of innocence to George Floyd and guilt for Derek Chauvin—a transfer he never could imagine would take place. We will see in later chapters how slipping into an alternate reality facilitates seeing violence as justified is not new.

As much as we can drill down and point to several ways the death of George Floyd and its aftermath ushered in an unprecedented torrent of activity globally that reverberates to this day, we cannot ignore the reality that, in many ways, things are not different; they are the same as they have always been. The most compelling reason in my mind why this is true is precisely related to one of the reasons its impact is so unprecedented. The reason why the killing of George Floyd has been monumental is because of its impact built off of the murders of Ahmaud Arbery and Breonna Taylor, but its connection to those murders confirms that his death is inextricably tied to a legacy of state or community-sanctioned violence that scapegoats black people. His murderous demise shows us new revelations, but many of those revelations are situated in the long lineage of violent deaths of black men and women at the hands of police officers, it's just that it took a particularly blatant, gruesome circumstance to bring those revelations to the forefront. Case in point, I remember where I was and how I felt when Rodney King, Trayvon Martin, Michael Brown, and Freddie Gray were killed. When I saw George Floyd's murder, it triggered a different response that helped sharpen my understanding of the other murders of unarmed black bodies in a way that I hadn't understood previously.

In almost all the other cases, detractors were able to point to some misstep by the black victim, which gave cover for the police officers to feel threatened and use excessive force. In Rodney King's assault, he kept trying to get up; with Michael Brown the police officers stated he charged at them; with Amadou Diallo, he reached for his wallet and the officers thought he was reaching for a gun; with Tamir Rice, it was the "brandishing" of a toy gun; for Philando Castille it was reaching for his identification in the glove compartment; for Breonna Taylor, it was the firing of a shot by the boyfriend in reaction to police officers executing a no-knock warrant, that officers clung to for cover. But in the case of George Floyd, the officers had no element to point to as to how George Floyd was an imminent threat to their lives as he lay on the ground face down, legs pinned down, and hands handcuffed behind his back. The viciousness of his execution raises the question . . . if law enforcement officers can cavalierly murder someone who clearly wasn't a threat, who can deny that in other cases where cops gave justifications, those are possible decoys to cover the real issue of the willingness of police officers to use their platform as a means to uphold systemic racism? In some cases, it may be malicious; in other cases, it's a realization that white privilege is real and emblematic in America. The stark contrast between how cops handle encounters with white persons versus how Derek Chauvin callously discarded George Floyd, is part a central reason why his murder has become a *Kairos* moment in time; a time of reckoning that most of us could never have predicted even if we had known the facts ahead of time.

As I stated in the introduction, the death and aftermath of George Floyd in my mind, function in ways that show their undeniable connection to the legacy of police brutality in America as well as the global dehumanization of black and brown people as an effect of racism. When I use the word aftermath, I am specifically referring to how multiple communities responded to the death of George Floyd in the form of protests, riots and looting. In other words, just as the death of George Floyd created a familiar flashpoint in time because of its link to the legacy of the death of black and brown people by law enforcement for centuries, so also the aftermath from George Floyd's death links to the legacy of protests against police brutality.

But before I get to how the aftermath is connected to legacy, I first want to be intentional about connecting the brutal killing of George Floyd to the legacy of police brutality in this country. Let me explain why it's important to analyze these elements in this sequence. A certain segment of our population—not all of one race or political stripe—seems to routinely forget that the protesting, rioting and looting are the effect, not the root cause of civil unrest and moral decay in our society. These responses to the killings are the consequences of what Dr. Cornel West calls "A Broken System, A Failed Experiment," and yet when it comes to the killing of people who look like me by law enforcement, some have developed the habit of neglecting to focus on the nature of the use of lethal force, and instead shift to the effects of the response of the killing. The net effect of such behavior is at best a glossing over of despicable behavior of police officers, who can miraculously maintain composure and take Dylann Roof to go get a burger after he was suspected of killing multiple people in a church. But the moment a black person reaches for his documents, is jogging along a road, is asleep in their own home, wears a hoodie, runs away, is on the ground face down in handcuffs, he or she is a threat, such that lethal force is deemed justified. At worse it is the sanctioning of the irrational principle that cars, homes, commercial buildings, and the goods and services those entities provide are profoundly more valuable than the human life that was snuffed out. Equally worse is the deliberate attempt to highlight the criminality of the actions of the responders of the killing (protestors), rather than put such behavior in its proper context as a reaction to the criminal behavior of those who thought it not robbery to take human life from an unarmed individual. Whenever a person wants to start a conversation about these incidents, gives a one-sentence disclaimer (e.g., although I am not condoning the killing of unarmed Americans), but then suddenly wants to focus on the aftermath, I have no problem telling them that justice requires first paying proper attention to the root cause, the privilege of cops to hide behind qualified immunity, the militarization of the police force and their penchant to function as judge, jury, and executioner when it comes to folks who look like me—then we can discuss the response.

Even in focusing on the murder of George Floyd, you also have some who would have us believe that rather than focus on the behavior of the police officers, the appropriate thing to do is to sift through the victim's history in order to (discover and) expose their criminality, which becomes the basis for minimizing or justifying the deadly force used against them. They would have us focus on attempts to create a legacy of criminality in each case, conducting oppositional research justifying why due process of law should be excused and violence sanctioned . . . even though neither the Constitution, nor the laws of any State, territory, nor district of the United States permit excusing the due process of law. Again, this is another attempt to find a scapegoat and divert attention away from the root cause . . . systemic racism. The obsession of a sizable percentage of white America, and others who have been bought off by them, to paint with a broad brush all black individuals who find themselves caught up in these horrific cases of police brutality comes from a belief that somehow, they must be criminals deserving to be scapegoats. The origin of scapegoat, its use in scripture and its application for our dehumanization will be discussed in much greater detail in chapters two through five. But in this chapter, I am focusing on the murderous scapegoating first, and its numerous connections to other factors regarding the dehumanization of black and brown bodies, and then afterwards, move to talking about the aftermath.

The agonizing murder of George Floyd was not some isolated case. From the very beginning, when I first learned about it, I immediately situated it as connected to Ahmaud Arbery who was murdered by a former cop, Breonna Taylor, who was shot in her own home by police officers, and Christopher Cooper, who was victimized by a white woman weaponizing her privilege to call the police and falsely accusing him of threatening her. The mere proximity in terms of chronology of these racially charged incidents (Arbery on February 23, Taylor on March 20, and Cooper on May 25, the same day as George Floyd), compelled me to link them together and recognize that the aftermath to George Floyd's murder was influenced by a culmination of violence against black bodies rather than that one act.

Not only were all three linked in proximity in terms of chronology, but all three involved unarmed black people being unjustifiably victimized reportedly due to white aggression based on fear. Jogging in a neighborhood stoked fear. Sleeping in one's own bed stoked fear (no-knock warrant). Being dark and tall, stoked fear (George Floyd). Even requesting that a white woman abide by park regulations and leash her dog stoked fear (Christopher Cooper).

In linking George Floyd to the long legacy of police brutality against black people, I am tempted to chronicle the list of black victims whose names have become too familiar in American culture over the past couple of decades, but to do so would inflict gross injustice on the thousands of lesser-known, yet equally significant victims of police brutality. While some might consider Rodney King a seminal figure in the legacy of police brutality against blacks, he is justifiably noteworthy not because he represents the first black person known to be physically attacked by law enforcement in recent history, but because his attack was one of the earliest videotaped by a bystander for the world to see. It was that recording that helped society understand how a videotape of police assaulting blacks (despite precious examples of such snippets of similar violence caught on tape during the civil rights movement) could instantly galvanize people to act.

The reality is law enforcement has been using violence to prey upon black and brown bodies since the very first police department was established in Boston in 1838. At first, the communities most targeted by harsh tactics were recent European immigrants. But, as African Americans fled the horrors of the Jim Crow south, they too became the victims of brutal and punitive policing in the northern cities where they sought refuge. In 1929, the Illinois Association for Criminal Justice published the Illinois Crime Survey. Conducted between 1927 and 1928, it revealed that although African Americans made up just five percent of the area's population, they constituted 30 percent of the victims of police killings. The disparity between the percentage of black people in America compared to the overrepresentation in police killings has always revealed the hidden agenda of the culture of police departments, nevertheless, despite police brutality's ugly history in America, the aftermath of George Floyd's murder is unique.

As a person of faith, I must note that this finite space in time so as to be opportune is in reference to the reality of humans, not the reality of God. That is because we live within the four dimensions and as such, are governed by time, but God is not: "For a thousand years in your sight are like yesterday when it is past, or like a watch in the night" (Psalm 90:4). When we understand how God's creation is situated in time, but God the Creator dwells in a reality that transcends time, it enlightens our perspective of what it means when the Son of God proclaims, in Mark 1:15: "The time is fulfilled, and the kingdom of God has come near; repent, and believe in the good news." For the famous German theologian Paul Tillich, "Kairos is the point in history when time is disturbed by eternity." Just five days after George Floyd was murdered, I preached the sermon: "I Can't Breathe, so God Breathe into Me," for the last Sunday in May. However, when it came time to prepare to bring another word for the first Sunday in June, in tribute to George Floyd and the aftermath that had ensued, it was abundantly clear: God used that moment in time, to institute *Kairos*, to break into our existence in a special way, to facilitate new possibilities, to compel folks of diverse racial and ethnic stripes to reimagine their realities, and to reassert the relevancy of Holy Scripture for our political, social and spiritual constructs. By June 7, 2020, I believed "mine eyes had seen the glory of the coming of the Lord." That is what I mean when I say we are in a *Kairos* moment in time.

Initially, what I found amazing about this moment, this *Kairos*, is its undeniable tie with the dehumanization of black and brown bodies throughout history, especially since 1619. From slavery (forced labor), to Black Reconstruction (black codes, sharecropping), to Jim Crow (lynching, race riots), to the civil rights movement (assassinations, protest clashes with police), to the unleashing of drugs in impoverished neighborhoods (crack, heroin), to the war on drugs (criminalizing of drug use), to the New Jim Crow (mass incarceration/prison industrial complex), to the 1992 crime bill (crack/cocaine powder disparity, three strikes you're out), to the killing of unarmed minorities on camera by law enforcement, George Floyd's murder was a watershed moment in a continuum of events spanning 402 years, that paints a haunting narrative of startling clarity.

As a seminarian who took courses on different methodologies for biblical interpretation, I was taught to resist the notion of obsessing over a singular text or verse of scripture, but instead, to always search for context which illumines and clarifies meaning. I know that seeing a verse in its greater context often has significant influence over the verse's meaning. And conversely, to focus on gleaning understanding of a verse of scripture solely in isolation is to be avoided if possible because it often renders a skewed interpretation. Accurate interpretation instead requires considering all the factors and their relationship to each other. This chapter has been an attempt to treat this *Kairos* moment as I would a single Bible verse or text, and dutifully appreciate its relationship to a broader context. The power that comes from this moment in time partially comes from its undeniable connection to the long horrific legacy of the dehumanization of black and brown bodies. One of the incendiary flashpoints that come to life when one connects this *Kairos* moment to the legacy of dehumanization of black and brown people, is that all the talk about racial progress in significant ways has been just that, talk. Yes, the George Floyd murder and its aftermath mark a distinctive moment in history, but in essence, nothing has changed. And there is a possibility that if it hasn't changed—even after the brilliance of W.E.B. DuBois, the charisma of Martin Luther King, the relentlessness of a Harriet Tubman, or the class of President Barack Hussein Obama—despite updated policies, consent decrees and implicit bias training, and protestors from diverse backgrounds having united to march against police brutality, things may never change. Having that big picture is incredibly informative and tremendously disturbing, but simultaneously empowering, nonetheless.

While we should recognize the power of connecting this *Kairos* moment to the murders of Ahmaud Arbery and Breonna Taylor, and to countless others as well as to the broader legacy of dehumanization of us by sanctioned power (i.e., authorized by government and society to use deadly force when it is deemed justified), we must not allow our connecting to undervalue and undermine the distinct power held within the killing of George Floyd. Because we have seen this story play out over and over in a plethora of modes all leading to the same end, society has become especially skillful at desensitizing us regarding our own destruction. Case in point, the more we string the narrative, the more normative it becomes in our way of life. As necessary as it is to connect the dots and not see this moment in isolation, we cannot allow the bombarding and totality of dehumanization spanning over four centuries and counting, to dull our moral and psychic outrage. Praise God, some critical elements of departure have allowed us to both see connection and distinction in the death of George Floyd, so let us pivot to those distinctions now.

CHAPTER 2

Leviticus 16: God's Response to Violent Scapegoating in Genesis 37 and Understanding the Nuanced Nature of Atonement

As much as it was necessary to lay the foundation for this work by uncovering how the present *Kairos* moment is both uniquely distinctive by creating new possibilities not accessible prior to now, and at the same time, how it is inextricably tied to a horrid, dastardly legacy of racial violence inflicted on black and brown bodies since 1619, the goal of this book is to ascertain where is God in the midst of all this chaos? What is God saying to us? Can God's Word as revealed in scripture give us enlightenment and direction during these troubling times?

Leviticus is the book of the first five books of the Bible (a section often referred to as the Pentateuch or Torah) that specifically deals with the dissemination and explanation of laws for the Israelites "to live by, as a way for them to express their devotion and to maintain their holiness." God made a covenant with His people and part of the stipulations in the covenant requires His people to live holy even as God is holy. Since no human being is perfect, God mandated the Levite priests to maintain devotion to Him by conducting worship rituals "for officiating, observing purification, and administering in the sanctuary," that set them apart from others, and God mandated all Israelites to obey animal sacrifice laws that paid for their sins.

Leviticus is widely agreed to be the recorded laws Moses received from God to give to the Israelites, but a growing segment of biblical scholars contend that what we have written in the Bible could easily have been the spoken words of Moses given to someone else, who eventually took the time to put on record. Written between 1440 and 1240 BCE, the content of Leviticus is basically divided into two parts; chapters 1 through 16, addressed to priests, "provides directions concerning acts of officiating and purifying . . . while the second division (chapters 17-27) emphasizes holiness among all Israelites." To be in fellowship with a holy God is the primary reason behind the laws, but they are also to help Israel embody its global calling to communicate the holiness of God through its obedience to God's sacrificial system.

Leviticus 16 is the key chapter that contains this biblical notion of scapegoating within God's sacrificial system of atonement, and I've come to the conclusion that when we pry beneath the surface, the Holy Spirit illumines the biblical narrative in ways that distinctly inform our present-day context. Before I dive into the significance of the scapegoat ritual, it is important to situate the ritual associated with the scapegoat within the larger context of Yom Kipper. Yom Kipper, also known as the Day of Atonement, is the most significant date in all the Jewish calendar. Falling in the month of Tishrei (September or October in the Gregorian calendar), it marks the culmination of the 10 Days of Awe, a period of introspection and repentance that follows Rosh Hashanah, the Jewish New Year. According to tradition, it is on Yom Kippur that God decides each person's fate, so Jews are encouraged to make amends and ask forgiveness for sins committed during the past year. The holiday is observed with a 25-hour fast and a special religious service.

On the day of Yom Kippur, the high priest (Kohen Gadol) had to follow a precise order of services, sacrifices, and purifications (or otherwise face the same fatal punishment for disobedience that Aaron's sons did in Leviticus 16:1). Before entering the tabernacle, Aaron was to bathe and put on special garments (verse 4), then sacrifice a bull for a sin offering for himself and his family (verses 6, 11). The blood of the bull was to be sprinkled on the Ark of the Covenant. Next, Aaron was to bring two goats, one to be sacrificed to God "because of the uncleanness and rebellion of the Israelites, whatever their sins have been" (verse 16), and its blood was sprinkled on the Ark of the Covenant. The other goat was used as a scapegoat, a vessel in the form of a live animal for carrying the weight of the iniquities of the people of God and removing those iniquities from the community. Aaron placed his hands on the head of the scapegoat, confessed over it the rebellion and wickedness of the Israelites, and sent the goat out with an appointed man who released it into the wilderness (verse 21). The goat carried on itself all the sins of the people, which were forgiven for another year (verse 30). Then Aaron went into the tabernacle to remove the linen garments he had put on to go into the holiest of holies, he washed himself, put his garments back on "and offered his burnt offering and the burnt offering of the people, and make atonement for himself, and for the people (verse 24)." Next, Aaron burned the fat of the sin offering on the altar, while the one who was tasked with leading the scapegoat out into the wilderness comes back, washes his clothes, bathes himself in fresh water and returns to the camp. As the blood of the bullock and the goat which had been offered in the special expiatory sacrifices of the day had been carried out within the sanctuary (verses 14, 15), their bodies had to be burnt outside the camp (verse 27). After washing his clothes and bathing in fresh water, Aaron was qualified to come (back) into the camp.

In response to God's call for the community to show solidarity in repenting for their sins and seeking atonement ("you shall afflict your souls" verse 29 and 23:27), Yom Kippur has become the day when Jews focus on their individual and collective spiritual well-being and set their physical requirements by adhering to five specific practices they abstain from (eating and drinking, wearing leather, bathing and shaving, anointing ourselves with oils or lotions, and having sexual relations). To date, fasting (not eating or drinking) is the most familiar custom practiced on Yom Kippur.

Leviticus 16 is considered the climactic chapter within the whole book, and Yom Kipper is considered the most important set of rituals in all of the Pentateuch because they depict the sacrificial expiation (redemption) for all sin and purification from all uncleanliness for the tabernacle, the priests, the altar, and the people. Given the significance of Yom Kippur even to this day, the distinctive ritual of atonement commemorated by millions of Jews annually, which is birthed out of biblical law spelled out in Leviticus 16, numerous scholars have weighed in on understanding the rituals as they exist in the text and how it came to be. Upon discovering Leviticus 16 in preparation to preach at Family of Faith A.M.E. Church in St. Thomas, USVI, the Sunday after George Floyd's death, I did some moderate exegetical research so that I could speak on the chapter with some authenticity for the sermon "From Scapegoats to Lambs," but the scope of this endeavor here demands a more comprehensive study of the chapter and the nature of the scapegoat ritual in particular.

To lay out how the scapegoat ritual in Leviticus 16 possibly connects with the chronic tragedy of unarmed black and brown bodies being dehumanized and victimized by entities sanctioned by the community to protect it (i.e., law enforcement), we cannot go much further without getting a good sense of what this text is saying. I will attempt to do that by laying out what prevailing biblical scholars have said about this scripture. The problem is so much has been written about Leviticus 16, and not all of it is relevant for our discussion here. Therefore in order to narrow our scope, I want to focus on four major issues that help to begin to build the bridge from God's Word written thousands of years ago, to the ongoing use of excessive force by law enforcement in America on people of color and especially black men. Those four issues are: the disputed origin of Leviticus 16, the numerous meanings of the word atone, how each of the three rituals in Leviticus 16 (sin offering, scapegoat ritual, and burnt offering) function to atone the people of God from their sins, and the numerous interpretations of what the Bible refers to as scapegoat. With each of the four issues, I will state the stance of the prevailing experts, and then I will unveil where I stand in relationship to the scholars and why. At the end of addressing each of the four issues, I will summarize and conceptualize a distinct interpretive commentary of what God has shown me about how these four issues shed light on how Leviticus 16 informs the role of police brutality in our society today.

Disputed Origins of Leviticus 16

There is a school of biblical interpretation that uses as one of its tools the comparison of biblical texts with other Ancient Near Eastern documents and narratives prevalent during the time the books of the Bible were written. They do this to detect and discern whether extra-biblical factors may have influenced the distinct way in which biblical authors penned their books. To that end, when you look at the breadth and width of current biblical scholarship regarding Leviticus 16, the overwhelming majority of interpretive experts believe that in varying degrees, Ancient Near Eastern sources concerned with the disposal of evil were used as source material with extensive modifications to construct the rituals of individual and communal atonement of sins in this weighty text. While the list of scholars who land on this side is numerous, one of the standout most exhaustive studies that support this thesis is *The Disposal of Impurity: Elimination Rites in the Bible and in Hittite and Mesopotamian Literature,* by David P. Wright. This work meticulously compares the rituals in Leviticus 16 with similar aspects found in Near Eastern impurity elimination rites. The one major assumption that this work and other scholars make in studying the biblical ritual is that Leviticus 16 has a long and complicated history. This assumption fuels the justification that Near Eastern sources influenced the making of the atonement rituals in Leviticus 16.

On the other side of the ideological spectrum stand two scholars, Calum Carmichael and Howard Cooper. A biblical and Near Eastern literature professor and a Reformed Rabbi respectively have both written notable works that suggest a completely different impetus for the construction of the scapegoat ritual featured in Leviticus 16. Instead of siding with the notion that the making of the atonement rituals in Leviticus 16 is the result of a long, complicated history of modifying Near Eastern sources, these two have made a compelling case for understanding the scapegoat ritual on this Day of Atonement in Leviticus 16 to be heavily influenced by the story of Joseph and his brothers in Genesis 37.

As a refresher on that narrative text, Jacob is the father of twelve sons, eleven of whom grow to despise the one, Joseph, the one their father has shown favor over the others. The resentment of the eleven, because of the preferential treatment by their father, grows into a wickedness such that they feel justified in violently eliminating him from the family. The brothers conjure up a scheme to deceive their own father of his favorite son's demise by using a bloodstain on a coat to cover up their insidious agenda of assaulting and banishing their own flesh and blood. At first glance, this story seems juicy enough on its own merits, but one may ask the relevant question: what is it about this narrative that makes a compelling case connecting this biblical soap opera in Genesis 37 to divine legislation for cleaning up corruption and sin both in the temple proper and in the community in Leviticus 16?

First is the reality that, while Moses lived 400 years after Joseph—and this somewhat explains why the law given to Moses in Leviticus doesn't specifically mention the scapegoating narrative of Joseph and his brothers—the author of the Book of Jubilees, a pseudepigraphal document that is said to have been created during the time of Joseph, does insert the creation of Day of Atonement into his presentation of the story of Joseph in Genesis 37. He literally suggests that Joseph's brothers should institute a process of expiation that includes a goat because of their transgressions: "They should make atonement for themselves with a young goat . . . on the tenth of the seventh month, once a year, for their sins; for they had grieved the affection of their father regarding Joseph his son" (Book of Jubilees 34, 18). The brothers used a scapegoat to get them in a world of mess, so the author of Jubilees recommended that they use a goat to get them out of their mess. Centuries later, the law of Leviticus channels the recommendation of Jubilees in instituting a Day of Atonement that incorporated the use of a scapegoat.

The second connection between Genesis 37 and the scapegoat ritual in Leviticus 16, is closely related to the first, the source of the blood. As the story is told, Reuben literally saved Joseph's life, because the initial consideration was for the brothers to kill him. After insisting his life be spared, they stripped him of his long robe, threw him into a pit temporarily, and eventually sold him to the Ishmaelites who took Joseph to Egypt. To create the perfect alibi, Jacob's sons killed a goat; and used the blood of the goat to stain the long robe belonging to Joseph. When Jacob saw the blood of the goat on the robe he had given Joseph, he surmised that a wild animal must have killed his beloved son and torn him to pieces. The slaughtered goat, whose blood becomes the pawn, the means to deceive, in Hebrew is called a *s' ir iyizzim* (Genesis 37:31). Not coincidently, the goats in the scapegoat ritual of Leviticus 16 are also called *s'ir iyizzim*. In Leviticus 16, one goat is given as a sin offering to the Lord and is killed. The other goat's life is spared, but it is banished; sent away to "Azazel," to the wilderness. The same *s'ir iyizzim* blood that is the agent of deceit in Genesis 37, becomes the blood that atones in Leviticus 16!

Thirdly, in Genesis 37, there is a confession of sin by Joseph's brothers, "the first ever communal confession in biblical history," who ultimately have to plead for forgiveness from Joseph. In Leviticus 16, the community through the high priest is charged with confessing/placing the sins of the community onto the scapegoat. Later in this chapter, I will articulate more forcefully about the importance of confession as it relates to atonement drawing from this aspect of the bond between the two scriptures.

Fourth, the casting or sending away of Joseph first into the pit in the wilderness and eventually into slavery distinctly aligns with the banishing of the scapegoat into the wilderness in the scapegoat ritual in Leviticus 16:21-22. Just as the scapegoat carries the truth about the wickedness of his brothers' actions and agenda away from public exposure, so too the scapegoat in Leviticus 16 disperses the sins of the community, which have been placed on its head by the high priest, to conceal and transfer them away from the community's atmosphere. For Carmen Carmichael, "it is this aspect of the process that provides the most remarkable link between law and story. To be sure, the brothers are deceitfully and wrongfully shifting their wrongdoing to the goat, whereas in the (scapegoat) ritual (in Leviticus 16), their descendants are openly and honestly having the goat remove theirs." Furthermore, the killing of the goat by Joseph's brothers and the false narrative of the killing of Joseph by the goat align with the slaughtering of the goat given to God as a sin offering in the scapegoat ritual in Leviticus 16. In Genesis, evil uses violence to purge an unwanted entity thought to contaminate the community (group of brothers), in Leviticus 16, violence is used to cleanse the inner sanctum, and to decontaminate (by physical removal) the community from sin.

Fifthly, Professor Carmichael spells out that the evil that the brothers of Joseph have done is not akin to individual wrongdoing. This somewhat contrasts with the analysis of Howard Cooper, who compared the sins of the brothers with the sin of Cain, in that the brothers failed to own the responsibility of being their brother's keeper. I will not try to minimize Cain's egregious act of murder and his denial of wrongdoing, but while it set into motion a chain reaction the likes of which we are still grappling with today, the sins of Joseph's brothers against him facilitate the spreading of evil on multiple levels. Not only did they do wrong, but they also tried to build an elaborate scheme to cover it up. They lied, they violated and misused convenient tools at their disposal to accomplish their goal, which ultimately was to dishonor their own father and deny him a relationship with his son. Accordingly, Carmichael agrees with Reformed Rabbi Jacob Milgrom, who sees the atonement rituals of Leviticus as a comprehensive system of processes not designed to alleviate individual wrongdoing, but to address offenses that have produced impurity that affect the inner sanctum, and these wanton, unrepented sins done by the community can only be appropriately mitigated and expiated once a year on the Day of Atonement.

For me, the multitude and strength of the connections between Genesis 37 and the scapegoat ritual of Leviticus 16 tip the scale in my belief that the latter is birthed out of a divine command to address the former. In other words, I agree with Cooper and Carmichael that the bond between Genesis 37 and the scapegoat ritual in Leviticus 16 is practically undeniable with the dramatic narrative between Joseph and his brothers ingeniously informing the didactic, instructional law for communal atonement crafted centuries later. I am compelled to add some intriguing caveats to their brilliant uncovering of this relationship between the texts. Looking at divine law through the prism of a juicy soap opera gives the law meaning and significance that otherwise would be difficult to discern. My definition of a scapegoat prior to uncovering the Genesis text was simply characterized around notions of blaming someone else for one's own sins. With Genesis 37 as a frame of reference, my understanding of scapegoating has sharpened exponentially. Now I have customized my own reality of scapegoating to mean: (1) to use something or someone as a means to justify, make right, or atone for that which otherwise is unjustifiable or unrighteous; (2) to use something or someone to cover, hide, or get rid of one's own wrongdoing by forcibly transferring the wrongdoing from oneself onto another entity. This revised definition will certainly be helpful as we move to understand how biblical scapegoating informs societal dehumanization in the form of police brutality in the United States and I owe a debt of gratitude to Genesis 37 for it.

My last observation in relationship to the origins of Leviticus 16, with its connection to Genesis 37, hearkens back to three words I used in the previous paragraph. In both definitions of scapegoating, I began with the stipulation, to manipulate "something *or someone* . . ." Cooper and Carmichael do a great job of explaining how the goat functions to transfer wrongdoing away from Joseph's brothers to the goat. The reality is, when you apply my definition of scapegoating from above, Joseph himself functions as a scapegoat also. It is the disappearance and mistreatment of Joseph that functions to do a host of things: (1) to make Jacob consider focusing on loving the rest of his sons equally (versus to favoring Joseph over them). In other words, making Jacob do right by them (they were not feeling having to play second fiddle to Jacob's love for Joseph), is how they justify wronging Joseph; (2) Joseph's absence functions with the presence of the goat's blood on the long robe not only to transfer guilt from the brothers to the goat (Genesis 37:33) but also from the brothers to Jacob. The text tells us that it is Jacob who beckons Joseph to go find his brothers (Genesis 37:13-14), and the text implicitly shows us the depth of Jacob's sorrow when he learns of Joseph's demise. Any parent who loves their child would certainly tend to blame themselves if harm came to their beloved child as a result of said child following the directions of the parent. Therefore, the scapegoating of Joseph by his brothers functions to transfer responsibility from them to Jacob. Finally, it is not just the goat that is innocently mistreated (i.e., killed), it is Joseph who after being thrown into the pit is sold to Midianites merchantmen for 20 pieces of silver, and then eventually sold to Potiphar, an officer of Pharaoh in Egypt. That the goat in Genesis embodies the very definition of scapegoating seems obvious upon reflection; but the reality is, Joseph is forced to function as a scapegoat too. The goat's blood and Joseph's mistreatment must work hand in hand for the effective transfer of blame to take place. Having flushed out the origin of the scapegoat ritual in Leviticus 16, let us now transition to understand the numerous meanings of the Hebrew word for atone in Leviticus 16.

If there is a weakness or critique to looking at Genesis 37 as the impetus to the scapegoat ritual in Leviticus 16, it is that despite the multiple sins which piled upon each other to create a major scandal, the brothers came clean and confessed their sins to Joseph, which facilitated a reconciliation between the brothers. One could make the argument that the reconciliation between Joseph and his brothers in Genesis nullifies the need for a (scapegoat) ritual to address or mitigate the brothers' wrongdoing(s).

Let me state my reasons as to why I believe a creditable, compelling case can be made against the brothers' atonement despite Joseph's willingness to reunite and bond with them. There is controversy over whether the brothers confessed to their father what they did to Joseph. The confession of sin is a critical piece of atonement, yet there is no mention of a confession by Joseph's brothers to their father in scripture. However, there is every reason to believe that the brothers would be tempted not to tell their father Jacob what they did to his favorite son unless they absolutely were put into a position where they had to do so. At the end of Genesis 45, we see where Joseph has cleverly forced the hand of his brothers to go back to Canaan from Egypt, share with Jacob that not only is Joseph alive, but that because of the famine, Jacob and all the families of the brothers needed to gather their belongings and relocate to Egypt because the famine was going to last another five years. ". . . so that you and your household, and all that you have, will not come to poverty" (Genesis 45:11b). Ironically, as they leave to start their journey back home, Joseph tells his brothers, "Do not quarrel along the way." If the lie about Joseph's death told to their father did not exist, there would be no reason for the brothers to quarrel, and Joseph's command is an indication to the brothers that he knows of their guilt despite him revealing himself and embracing them prior to sending them back to Canaan. The text lets us know that when they get back home, they tell Jacob Joseph is alive and rules over Egypt, the news of which their father is cynical initially, but when they told Jacob all the words of Joseph (who never told them to expose their sin) combined with Jacob seeing the wagons and provisions Joseph had arranged to go back with the brothers, then Jacob believed. The language of Genesis 45:27 signals Jacob's willingness to put the past behind him and get on with the new possibilities presented by this good news. Seeing their father's spirit revived without any mention of a confession, it is logical to ascertain that the brothers never felt a need to do so. While they acknowledged their wrongdoings and repented (to Joseph), telling the truth to Jacob would only have caused him headache. Although Dr. Terence E. Fretheim from the New Interpreter's Bible Commentary concedes that Genesis 50 is the only text in which Jacob gives a clear indication that he knows what the brothers did to Joseph, if it were true, one must ask the question why the author of Genesis omits that juicy detail from an already spellbinding drama? Whether Jacob discovers on his own, or suspects and then commands his sons to come clean, those elements would have added significant material to this narrative. Without such details and knowing the lengths to which Joseph's brothers went to conceal their wrongdoing, Fretheim's conclusion that the brothers' report (in Genesis 50) to Joseph is factual (i.e., Jacob instructed Joseph to forgive his brothers) is on very shaky ground, and the concealment of the brothers' sins from the father remains problematic from an atonement perspective moving forward.

Furthermore, the phrasing of the language of scripture in Genesis 50 can easily support the notion that the agenda of Joseph's brothers, even in their confession, wasn't completely honorable. First of all, Joseph reveals his identity, alleviates the brothers of responsibility for being sold into Egypt by saying it is God, and not them who brought him to Egypt for a greater purpose in Genesis 45:7! So the question becomes, despite Joseph's brothers talking to him after Joseph kisses and wept over all his brothers in Genesis 45:15, if the brothers had fully reconciled in chapter 45, would there be a need for much of the narrative of chapter 50, where the brothers, fearful of Joseph because of Jacob's death, invoke Jacob in a multitude of ways to incite forgiveness from Joseph? In other words, if confession, forgiveness, and complete reconciliation had taken place in chapter 45, it would significantly lessen the significance of chapter 50. I will admit that fear of revenge from Joseph, especially after Jacob's death is quite plausible, such that the brothers may have felt a need to ensure their well-being despite a confession that possibly took place prior to the direct appeal in chapter 50. Fretheim compellingly recalls that Jacob's brother Esau waited until their father Isaac had passed before attempting to exact retribution on Jacob because his brother had stolen his birthright (Genesis 27:41). While I concede that this line of thinking holds some merit, one way the brothers could've tried to prevent such retribution is to get Jacob to speak to Joseph directly (versus through a messenger). His living words would surely carry more weight than a message sent from Jacob after he died. The problem was, such a strategy would require the brothers to confess to Jacob their sins; which again strengthens the notion that if they had told Jacob, either they wouldn't need to fear because Jacob may have shared and convinced them that Joseph's character was such that he never would exact revenge, or having told Jacob their wrongdoing, they would've been in a position to ask him to advocate for forgiveness on their behalf. The language of the narrative is framed by two things; the intense fear the brothers possessed because of Joseph's revenge, and the strategy to invoke Jacob (without having him do it directly while alive) as a means to mitigate the potential for Joseph's desire to exact revenge.

The brothers are acutely aware of the intense affection that existed between Jacob and Joseph. If I am right that Joseph's brothers never told Jacob about their sins, the devious invoking of Jacob's message to Joseph for the purpose of currying favor with him continues the piling on of the sins of the brothers on multiple levels. On one level, it demonstrates a refusal to come completely clean and be truly vulnerable with Joseph. This lack of transparency undercuts true reconciliation. Furthermore, if the brothers did not tell/confess Jacob their sins, the report of the brothers about Jacob's command for Joseph to forgive them MUST be a fabrication. Verses 15-17 of chapter 50 are written in such a way that one can easily interpret the actions of the brothers as using Jacob as a scapegoat to shield them from the wrath of Joseph. This whole scandal began with the brothers scapegoating Joseph to curry favor from their dad (they had hoped Jacob would now treat the siblings more equitably), but it crescendos with the brothers scapegoating Jacob (exploiting his death) to curry favor with Joseph! The message delivered to Joseph supposedly from Jacob via Joseph's brothers contains stern instructions for Joseph to forgive them, "Now therefore, please forgive the crime of the servants of the God of your father." The phrasing "the God of your father," is full of irony, as it could be a genuine father's plea for his son to recall the intimate relationship they shared, or it is a mischievous strategy of the brothers to use their dead father to pull on the heartstrings of Joseph. My negative reading of the brothers' agenda is further bolstered by the lack of a reference to Jacob in that last portion of verse 17 where the author of the narrative credits the message that Joseph receives comes from his brothers. If the brothers had a messenger tell Joseph (or told Joseph themselves as in the NRSV translation) what Jacob had precisely told them, the latter part of verse 17 strangely omits any credit to Jacob of what was spoken. To further the train of thought, does Joseph weep after receiving the message because he is happy his brothers finally desire reconciliation, because he knows he must comply with his father's wishes, or because he knows that his father would never send a message like that, understands exactly what the brothers have done, discerns their fear, yet sees God in the midst, and wants to move forward by putting this scandal in the past?

While Joseph demonstrates a love for his brothers that sees past their wrongdoings and refuses to embrace revenge, he never explicitly forgives them, and he shuns the brothers' attempt to placate his position as if he is a God/pharaoh. In summary, the brothers never explicitly confess, there is no record in the text that states they apologized, and Joseph never forgives, despite "Jacob" telling him twice to forgive his brothers. This is not to suggest that Joseph's love for his brothers is not genuine, or that his desire for reconciliation with his siblings is not sincere. Fretheim, while believing that the brothers' report to Joseph of Jacob's command for Joseph to forgive was not fabricated, he acknowledges that Joseph indeed shuns the need for forgiveness, and instead he chooses to center the whole event in terms of how God turned the agenda of evil into a divine blessing. To focus on being used for such a time as this to be a blessing to his brothers is unquestionably a remarkable thing for Joseph to do and reveals much about his character. But the reality remains, in terms of atonement for the sins of the brothers, Joseph seems adamant not to lord over his brothers, "Do not be afraid, am I in the place of God?" In a strange way, what seems to be percolating beneath the surface is the sentiment that while Joseph is fervently willing to put the scandal in the past, if my educated hunch that his brothers fabricated Jacob's message to Joseph is correct, God somehow must intervene to truly incite confession, repentance, and forgiveness so that divine exoneration can take place. To bring this full circle, the need for divine intervention because of these sins strengthens the reasoning why the scapegoat ritual in Leviticus 16 needed to be crafted to address individual and corporate atonement. The notion of how fear drives people to manipulate the truth and scapegoat others in order to hide evil intentions or to put themselves in a more favorable light is something that is painstakingly relevant to the use of excessive force that often results in the killing of unarmed black people by police in America today. My goal here is to show how those same sentiments were operating in full display for all to see in God's Word. And as we draw further insights from this initial premise in later chapters, I hope that seeing the scapegoat ritual in Leviticus 16 being a divine response to an infamous scapegoat scandal in Genesis 37-50, helps us see how God's Word is uniquely qualified to shed light on the mentality behind police brutality so that we can construct strategies for neutralizing its impact and move further toward its eradication.

The Numerous Meanings of Kipper/ Kippur "to Atone" in Leviticus 16

I read closely from a number of scholars who have a host of interpretations regarding the meaning of atone in Leviticus 16, but I found one scholar, Chandler Collins, in his groundbreaking thesis, *"Kipper and the Yom Kippur Rituals in the Discourse of Leviticus 16"* to be especially helpful. I will be honest in admitting that I am neither a master of Hebrew, Aramaic, or Greek language, but Collins is a biblical language specialist who in his master's thesis, draws from the top biblical scholars who have weighed in on the meaning of atone, who is extremely competent in explaining each expert's distinct position, objectively drawing out their strengths and weaknesses. The cherry on top is that his own positions are not wedded to one theological slant nor show favoritism to any one scholar over another. His perspective is an eclectic composite of slices of biblical interpretation from many scholars after having rigorously critiqued the perspective of each and deliberately choosing those positions that stand under intense scrutiny no matter who owns it. For these reasons, I will detail the salient points of his analysis of the different interpretations and add my own commentary where needed.

First and foremost, the customized blending of interpretations from various biblical scholars to form Collins' unique perspective comes from his belief that *kipper*, the word that is often translated to atone, is a complex Hebrew verb, having four distinct possibilities of meaning depending on the context: to cover, to ransom, to wipe/purge, and more generally to make atonement/expiation. In addition to the intense analysis of context as it relates to each occurrence of the Hebrew word for *kipper*, Collins examines etymology, the Hebraic prepositions used to accompany *kipper*, key occurrences of the verb in the Hebrew Bible and its Semitic cognates to attempt to shed light on the verb's meaning. At the end of the day, Collins points to the lack of clear evidence that shows the development of the base meaning of *kipper* as the reason why scholars are so varied in their interpretation of its meaning and why for now, we should work from the premise that *kipper* was polyvalent (i.e., having multiple meanings) by the earliest stages we have it in the Hebrew Bible.

According to Collins, the case for *kipper* meaning to cover is weak, with the only biblical occurrence found in Genesis 6:14, where the actual root KPR is found but not the identical word. Without getting too far in the weeds, while *kipper* and KPR share the same root, there are circumstances when the meanings are not identical and according to the OT linguistic scholars, this is one of those cases. Therefore, since this is the only occurrence of any variant of KPR found in the Bible that speaks to the meaning to cover, Collins is skeptical of the notion that *kipper* could mean "to cover." It is worth noting that Strong's Expository Concordance and Vines Expository Dictionary, widely used by students of the Bible globally, both associate *kipper* with the meaning to cover and cite Genesis 6:14 for evidence.

Next Collins examines the near-identical wording of Jeremiah 18:23 and Nehemiah 3:37 as evidence that *kipper* has the base meaning "to cover," a premise put forward by Yitzhaq Feder. Collins intensely analyzes the etymological factors of the Hebrew language for these verses and ultimately concludes that in the original language, the verbs in question in these respective verses cannot be proven to have identical meaning, despite both covering sin and wiping away sin enjoying special prominence in scripture. For our purposes here, it is significant whether the Hebrew word *kipper* found in Leviticus 16 has occurrences where its meaning could be rendered "to cover." While Collins may have a case about a lack of conclusive proof that the authors of the Bible equated "to cover" with "to wipe," that doesn't negate the very real possibility that there is some association between the two, and so as we move forward to attempt to understand *kipper* in Leviticus 16, we cannot divorce ourselves from the notion that when the text can be discerned to mean "to wipe/purge," an element of or some relationship to "to cover" could be embedded as well.

Given this potential connection between to cover and to wipe/purge, it seems relevant to explore the notion of "to wipe/purge" in the Bible and especially Leviticus 16. In his master's thesis, Collins draws upon the scholarship of Jacob Milgrom, who believes that "to cover" and "to wipe/

purge" are complementary, not contradictory in terms of relationship, Yithaq Feder, who doesn't see *kipper* meaning "to wipe" in Hebrew but does see *kipper* to mean "to purge" in Hebrew scripture, Richard Averbeck, who sees *kipper* as "to wipe/purge," and Baruch Levine, who sees *kipper* as meaning "to wipe" based on Genesis 32:21, which he interprets "to wipe away with wrath." Collins notes how Feder effectively dismantles Dr. Baruch A. Levine's interpretation, and therefore he dismisses Averbeck's organizing principle as a way of discerning the meaning of *kipper*, despite the fact that Averbeck comes to the right conclusion that *kipper* can mean "to purge." When I read this, I couldn't help but be reminded of my high school math days, where I would occasionally stumble upon the right answer despite using a flawed mathematical process. Collins notes that Averbeck believes *kipper* can take the meaning "to ransom" when it refers to "the overall effect of the action," thereby supporting Collins' assertion that *kipper* can take on different meanings depending on context. When Averbeck explains why, in Leviticus 16, the Hebrew word *kipper* even used with different prepositions could refer to "making atonement" for the temple, Collins believes that this may show how *kipper* may convey the idea of purging and ransoming intertwine in certain circumstances, particularly Leviticus 16.

Collins then focuses on the scholarship of Nobuyoshi Kiuchi and his interpretation of *kipper* as connected to appeasement/ransom. After also arguing that *kipper* is reflexive from his understanding of Lev. 10:17 (the priest bears the sin of the people via the offerings), Kiuchi proposes the rendering "to sacrifice oneself for appeasement," or "to sacrifice oneself" for *kipper*. While appreciative of the thoroughness of Kiuchi's analysis, Collins believes Kiuchi pushes too far when he argues that every occurrence for *kipper* renders the same, and instead posits that each sacrifice had its own historical uses before being incorporated into the tabernacle system and unique function within it, and therefore allowance must be made for each one to stand on its own and make atonement in a different way. "Each sacrifice can be a part of that system and have expiatory effects without each one having to accomplish expiation in the same way." Collins then effectively dismantles Kiuchi's interpretation of Leviticus 16:20 and asserts that *kipper* in that verse should be rendered "to purge."

Going forward, we should assume that as early as the Hebrew Bible was written, the meanings "to wipe/purge" and "to ransom/appease" already existed together in *kipper*. There is also the use of *kipper* to refer to the entire act of "making atonement" which seems to already be fallen into the verb at this time as well. It is possible that the broad sense of "making atonement/expiation" was a later development historically, but that could only be deduced on principle, not shown in texts. The only "Johnny come lately" is the meaning "to cover," which Collins believes does not have compelling evidence to suggest it existed in the earliest stages of Hebrew.

Since *kipper* occurs some 16 times in Leviticus 16, we would be irresponsible to not make some attempt to ascertain its meaning in the text. I believe, that while scapegoating is found in numerous places in the Bible, Leviticus 16 is the foundational scripture for the concept, because it seems to respond to the scapegoating found in the Genesis narrative with Joseph and his brothers, it prophetically points forward toward Jesus, and it enlightens some of our sociological behavior found in our communities today. Unfortunately, Collins, in gathering all the recent scholarship behind the meaning of *kipper*, discloses that its root meaning remains elusive due to a lack of evidence of its "diachronic development," which fosters diverse interpretations and rigorous debate. In seeing the potential for *kipper* meaning different or multiple things depending on context, and other factors, which appreciates the distinct scholarship of Collins, we are afforded an opportunity to access understanding and implications regarding scapegoating that shed valuable insight. I don't believe God to be one-dimensional; the Lord is well able and qualified to choose multiple ways to show us how to confront negative scapegoating (a la the Genesis narrative with Joseph and his brothers) as well as reconfigure it in ways that neutralize its nefarious agendas and usher in the facilitation of holiness (a la Leviticus 16).

The Functioning Atonement in the Three Rituals in Leviticus 16

The slaughtering of the bull and goat found in Leviticus 16 function as sin offerings designed to purge the community from sin. Collins believes that there are ten instances of *kipper* used in connection with the sin offerings in Leviticus 16. Three are used to purge the sancta (verses 20, 33 [2x]). Collins agrees with Milgrom that these occurrences of *kipper* should be translated "to purge," as he does in his commentary. The slaughtered goat purged the sancta, but the live goat was a dispenser of sin. While most scholars believe that the sin offerings purge or purify, they disagree greatly on whether they purge the sancta or the offerors. Blood rites do purge the sanctuary and its components while burning rites accomplish forgiveness for sins that the offeror bears. Collins believes along with Milgrom that the blood of the goat in the sin offering acts as a detergent that cleans the sancta from defilement. The verbs for "to cleanse" and "to purify" occur with the sin offering, whereas the verbs "to bear" and "to send" occur in connection with the scapegoat. Collins believes the two goats did not work in isolation from the bull goat which was slaughtered and eaten.

The high priest's confession of all the people's sins and their banishing from the camp assured them of his covenant commitment to them and his willingness to forgive them of their iniquities. It is clear that the sins of the people were loaded on the goat since the one who led it into the wilderness became unclean in that process. Therefore, the sending of the goat truly was a *kipper* act that removed the sins of the people that had accumulated throughout the year and purified them as a group. This rite combined with the purging effect of the sin offerings allowed YHWH to continue to dwell among an unholy people. Further, the confession of the high priest served as the foundation and impetus for the people's humbling of their own souls and seeking YHWH as a community. Therefore, while there is discontinuity between the scapegoat and slaughtered offerings (they both deal with different kinds of evils, etc.), I believe a careful read of the text shows that they did work together as a system to both purge the tabernacle complex and the community.

The scapegoat ritual functions to further purify by removing the iniquities from the community. Gane believes that the scapegoat ritual is a broad super-paradigm that includes all the sacrifices whose goal is "purification in the broad sense of removing moral faults and/or physical ritual impurities." This understanding according to Collins allows each ritual to function on its own but allows for both to be contributing to the same broad process of purification.

As we noted above, it is significant that the scapegoat is never referred to as a sin offering in the chapter although there were ample opportunities for the author to do so (see verses 10, 20-22, 26). Meanwhile, the goat for YHWH is referred to several times as a sin offering (verses 9, 15). These observations lead Collins to the conclusion that the original Hebrew in verse 5 that speaks to the function of atonement refers only to the one goat dedicated to YHWH. It should be translated: "for a sin offering." This means that of the two goats, only one was eventually designated as a sin offering. While Collins adopts Kiuchi's translation of verse 5, he believes the grammar of verses 9-10 has dealt a significant blow to Kiuchi's theory that the two goats work as one offering. This stance characterizes the goat for YHWH as the only sin offering, while the scapegoat is another kind of ritual altogether.

The RSV and ESV translate the result clause in the scapegoat ritual in ways that make the atonement act the confession of the priest rather than the sending of the goat. However, the text stresses the goat's bearing of sin away from the camp (verse 23), which suggests this is the atonement act in connection with the scapegoat rather than the priest's confession. Moreover, Aaron's confession does not require an animal if it is an atonement act by itself, so Collins believes. However, Collins prefers to translate this abstract sense of *kipper* in relation to the way the scapegoat makes atonement. Since it physically removes the sins of the Israelites away from the camp, the emphasis of *kipper* here is on expiation. Therefore, it should be translated to something like "to perform expiation," as Levine and Milgrom do.

But from my perspective, we must ask the corollary as well; can the sending away of the sins without the high priest's confession be an atonement by itself? Does the atonement in Leviticus 16 pertain to the scapegoating which occurs between Joseph and his brothers? The answer is an emphatic no. Atonement occurs because of the confession and the sending away of the sin. For me, this is one of the major departure points from Collins' work. For Joseph's brothers, the path of atonement and forgiveness required them confessing their sins to their brother . . . but does scripture speak to the notion of Joseph's brothers seeking atonement with their father who they deceived by means of the scapegoat? If not, it lends credence to why, in spite of their confession to Joseph, the lack of confession to Jacob along with other sins, required the scapegoat ritual in Lev. 16 to be instituted in the first place.

The burnt offerings function as a ransom to appease, entreat, or seek the favor of God. In the burnt offering section of Lev. 16, Collins believes that the Hebrew word for atonement *kipper* is best translated propitiation (which means to gain the favor of or appease). He agrees with Milgrom who thinks the basic goal of the burnt offering was entreaty. For example, he points to I Sam. 13:12 where Saul offered a burnt offering as a way to "seek the favor of." The entreaty of the offeror was caused by any number of situations such as "homage, thanksgiving, appeasement, [or] expiation." This gift-like nature of the burnt offering appears to also be its expiatory function. Averbeck notes, "The burnt offering carried an atoning effect as a gift that appeased or entreated God rather than as a literal cleansing procedure." The ransom was the main job of the burnt offerings and the main function of the sin offerings was to purge the sancta with the blood. Therefore, the texts about the sin offerings stress blood manipulation rather than the soothing aroma of its fat. This means that not only are the burnt offerings not subsumed under function of the sin offerings, but instead, that the fat of the sin offerings assumes the function of the burnt offerings. The burnt offering went up in smoke before YHWH as a sweet-smelling gift and functioned as a sort of ransom.

In verses 29-31 of Lev. 16, we have a subunit of the chapter summary in the form of a chiasm. Collins agrees with Milgrom regarding the chiastic structure of the subunit: Verses 29 and 31 envelop verse 30 and emphasize the importance of the people humbling themselves before YHWH and ceasing from work on the Day of Atonement. Verse 30 is the center, and hence, the emphasis of the chiasm.

This chiasm strengthens my personal belief that the confession of the sins by the high priest onto the scapegoat is just as fundamental to the nature of atonement as the sending away of the sins by the scapegoat. How? Since verse 30 emphasizes the importance of the people being made clean because they have humbled themselves before YHWH, one can easily make the case that in all of this chapter, the exposing and confessing of the sins of the community is the most humbling aspect of the rituals for the day. Kiuchi believes "Whether or not the ritual on the Day of Atonement achieved such a goal depended on whether the Israelites observe the command to *afflict their souls*." However, Collins believes that the structure of verse 30 presents the purification of the people as a completed action dependent only upon the high priest. Could it be that both are correct? The people humbled themselves by confessing their sins to the high priest, who in turn confessed the community's sins by placing the collective burden on the head of the goat. Then the goat is sent away into the desert/wilderness. Thus, the atonement comes from the people afflicting their souls by sharing their sins with the priest, who then himself personifies the ritual of atonement by following God's instructions to Moses. Again, I am not trying to say the confession aspect of the scapegoat ritual is more important than the scapegoat being sent away. I'm saying it is an essential part; for the sins to be sent away without confession prevents atonement just as confession without the sins being removed from the community also prevents repair of the broken relationship with YHWH.

According to Collins, verse 30 does not imply that everyone in the congregation repented of all their sins before YHWH, but that because of the priest's actions, he would overlook their sin and did not allow it to endanger his residency with them. Throughout the year, the people had jeopardized YHWH's holy presence in the camp and incurred His wrath by breaking His instruction, but now the slate had been wiped clean. Although this purification was automatic, the commands to the people in verses 29 and 31 are important because they were to spend the Day humbling themselves and fasting with the goal of internalizing what was being accomplished on their behalf. This analysis naturally raises the question as to what particular ritual verse 30 refers to that cleansed the people. The clue that helps us discern the answer is in verse 21, "Then he is to lay both hands on the head of the live goat and confess over it all the iniquities and rebellious acts of the Israelites in regard to all their sins. He is to put them on the goat's head and send it away into the wilderness by the hand of a man appointed for the task." How is the high priest capable of confessing over the goat all the iniquities and rebellious acts of the Israelites in regard to all their sins unless they all specifically tell him? This is the ultimate act of being humbled short of going to God directly and confessing. And ironically with Jesus as both our high priest/scapegoat 2.0, that is exactly what Christians are required to do today to achieve atonement. "If we confess our sins, He is faithful and just to forgive us our sins and cleanse us from all unrighteousness (Romans 10:9)." I pull from a completely different passage of scripture not to selectively construct a shoestring theology, but instead to show the consistency throughout the Bible that atonement requires confession, and the high priest's role is important, but so is the role of the people in laying bear their sins.

The Multiple Meanings of Scapegoat/Azazel in Leviticus 16

When it comes to the term Azazel, the word which has been interpreted to mean scapegoat since William Tyndale first used the term "scapegoat" in his 1530 translation of the Bible, I agree with Collins who believes that the designation Azazel speaks to the goat's function. There are three main theories which scholars propose for what Azazel is: (1) a destination the goat is destined to travel to that is characterized by rough, rocky terrain, (2) the going/sent away goat and (3) a demon-like figure to whom the goat is sent. Collins believes the structure of Lev. 16:8 treats both YHWH and Azazel as proper names. Many scholars thought that the goat was sent out to the desert, inhabited by demons and the goat was also interpreted by others as a demonic figure in the literature of Second Temple Judaism.

Collins rejects the notion that Azazel means a location and he rejects that it means the going away goat because of how Leviticus 16:10 is grammatically structured. He is strongly persuaded with how one goat is offered to God for a sin offering and the other goat is kept alive and sent to Azazel. Thus for him, and it would seem a number of scholars, Azazel represents the proper name of an entity, in this case, a demon, or angry god. Lester L. Grabbe in his article entitled *The Scapegoat Tradition: A Study in Early Jewish Tradition*, compares the Azazel of Leviticus 16 with the Asael of 1 Enoch, an ancient Hebrew apocalyptic religious text, ascribed by tradition to Enoch, the great-grandfather of Noah. Grabbe observes that the names Asael and Azazel are similar, that the punishment for both occurred in the desert, that sin was placed on each, and that the sending away of either resulted in the healing of the land.

Meanwhile, Roger De Verteuil stated in his scholarly journal *The Scapegoat Archetype* that the images of the satyr, the demonic Azazel, and the scapegoat seem to blur and fuse together, like a mirage in the desert air, revealing their "archetypal roots within the (mentality) of the Children of Israel." Carmichael, who is looking at Leviticus 16 through the lens of the scandalous scapegoating of Joseph by his brothers in Genesis, also attributes Azazel to being a personified figure of generalized evil (while astutely observing the connection between the goat of Joseph in the wilderness and the scapegoat of Leviticus 16 being sent away to the same location. "In this light, Azazel would symbolize (Joseph's brothers') malevolence of spirit." In terms of the minority of scholars who push for a more acute connection characterized by the goat and Azazel, Levine suggests that the Hebrew word for goat "ez" is represented in the word Azazel. Clearly, he is influenced by the LXX and the Vulgate, which see a reference to a goat when they read Azazel as a contraction of "ez"—"goat" and "azal"—"to go away." While Collins believes that Azazel is most probably the name of a demon, it should be noted that the priestly literature strips it of all its character, and it has no active role on the Day of Atonement. In my mind, while Collins suggests that there may be growing consensus around this third option, that Azazel means the demonic entity to which the scapegoat is sent, each of these three options for the potential meaning of Azazel has particular relevance as we consider how the characterization of Azazel informs the excessive force chronically inflicted by law enforcement on black and brown citizens.

CHAPTER 3

Reenvisioning Isaiah 53: Reinterpreting the Voices, Navigating the Theological Shift from Scapegoats to Lambs

Isaiah 53 is a most formidable, complex passage of scripture to navigate and appropriate for our 21st-century context. My initial inquiry into the nature of scapegoating after witnessing the murder of George Floyd did not lead me immediately to the Suffering Servant motif of Isaiah 53. But in diving into Leviticus 16, which ultimately led me back to Genesis 37-42, I began to understand that the leap from those Old Testament passages to Jesus' being scapegoated in the New Testament gospels is actually a progression foretold in the prophetic writings of Isaiah 53. The goat that was killed by Joseph's brothers in Genesis, which becomes reinvented as the sacrificial goat used for atonement in Leviticus 16, transforms into the human/nation scapegoat prophesied in Isaiah 53, before being the scapegoat personified in Jesus in the gospels. Not only does Isaiah 53 align with the scapegoat narratives of Genesis 37 and Leviticus 16, in so much that the themes of rejection, suffering bloodshed, the carrying of sins, being cast away, justice and atonement reappear, but the nature of suffering and atonement function in surprisingly fresh ways that compel me to characterize the mining of interpretive insights from Isaiah 53 in the journey towards Jesus' scapegoating not just as confirmation but also as a progression.

Apparently, Isaiah was not only the most helpful single book of the Old Testament in assisting the early church to understand the sufferings and crucifixion of the Christ, but Isaiah also provided help in understanding nearly every phase of Jesus' life, ministry, death, and resurrection. Given this reality; it makes sense to now take a substantive dive into the factors which specifically make the Suffering Servant poem of Isaiah 53 so relevant to the purpose of this work.

"Historically, Christians have interpreted Isaiah 53 as a Christological prophecy and, consequently, have drawn from this passage to develop accounts of (and responses to) Christ's suffering." What most Christians may not do, is track the ongoing research that members of the academy conduct on important scriptures like Leviticus 16 and Isaiah 53. Those who may have done some research, might be aware that one of the reasons Christians find this scripture so endearing is because of its Messianic overtones, but lesser known is the notion that there are a multitude of voices to navigate in this passage: the servant, the servants, and the nations. And to add another layer of complexity, the voice of the nations is portrayed through the servants, who not only transmit the messaging of the nations, but also have their own distinct yet not unrelated messaging that they articulate. "This poem represents the culmination of all that precedes and constitutes the decisive boundary line in the larger discourse (chapters 40-66), as the text moves from the achievement of the servant (40:1-52:11) to the work of the servants (54:1-66:24), which is an elaboration and ramification of that prior legacy." In other words, the servant speaks from chapter 48 through chapter 52:7-12, the servant dies at the end of chapter 52, chapter 53 chronicles a tribute conveying the immediate reaction of the servants and the nations to the servant's death, with chapter 54 having the servants picking up where the servant left off. Deciphering when the servants are speaking for themselves, versus when they are relaying the message of the nations is key to understanding Isaiah 53. A simple example that conveys what is at stake is when a family member dies, and multiple people get up to pay tribute to the deceased at the funeral. Knowing whether the person giving the tribute is representing themselves as part of a larger group, or whether they are reading and relaying a message from another group has profound implications on the hearers' understanding of the tribute and by extension, the sentiments of the messenger. In the present form of Isaiah 53, not only are multiple tributes to the deceased servant interwoven (one voice saying a line or two, followed by another voice, then the process repeating several times) into one large tribute in the form of a poem, but the voices don't explicitly tell you when they are speaking for themselves versus when they are articulating and passing along sentiments from a different group to which they do not belong. The lack of clarifying descriptors in the poem to help differentiate who is speaking (versus who is being represented) also fuels generations of readers to see themselves represented in the tribute, especially as we see Jesus embody the Suffering Servant on Calvary, becoming a light for the nations through His death and resurrection.

Even though Christians see the servant as Jesus, what helps us to come to a more nuanced, multi-layered interpretive approach to interpreting the text is to realize that the immediate readers of this second unit of Isaiah, chapters 40-66, would have had several entities who could qualify as servant. For some, the mentioning of servant would've had them envision the authors of this poem to be talking about Moses, who embodied Isaiah 53:12, because he not only bore the sins of a generation in the wilderness, but he also successfully interceded for God's people, which caused God to withhold judgment (Deuteronomy 9:25-29). Other readers of Isaiah 53 would have undoubtedly imagined Israel as the Suffering Servant and Isaiah 49:3 gives them justification for doing so. Seen from this perspective, the "servant's death is reckoned as representative of Israel's death and suffering at the hands of the nations." Thus, we have the Suffering Servant motif functioning on at least two levels; an individual death functioning as redemptive, on behalf of their servants, and the suffering and death of Israel, on behalf of the nations. We will posit the potential of at least one other creative mode of interpretation, informed through the lens of violent communal scapegoating that I believe is quite compelling.

Dr. Christopher Seitz registers the structure of the passage to be that the first nine verses of chapter 53 are characterized as the heart of the unit, where the servants describe the significance of the life and death of the Servant, bracketed by two similar units before (52:13-15) and after (53:10-12) that tell of the Servant's destiny. In the opening unit prior to the main section, "we see . . . an exaltation of the servant that entails the recognition of the nations . . ." Seitz entertains the notion that ritual cleansing of impurities may be indirectly alluded to in the opening unit of this three-part structure, but that what is most salient is that what God accomplishes through the suffering and death of the servant, both the servants and nations see, with the nations being astounded to the point where they have nothing to say.

As much as I appreciate Seitz's careful reading of Isaiah 53, one of the drawbacks of focusing exclusively on his analysis is his minimizing the reality that Isaiah 53 is a poem, and as such there are insights to be gained from the way in which the language and rhetoric of this poetic passage offers valuable insights. For example, Michael L. Barre, in his article entitled *"Textual and Rhetorical-critical Observations on the Last Servant Song (Isaiah 52:13-53:12),"* from the January 2000 edition of The Catholic Biblical Quarterly, observes that in the prologue (Isaiah 52:13-15), three adjectives "high, exalted, and lofty" in the thirteenth verse are followed by three exalted, human entities in verses fourteen and fifteen, the "many (or the great ones)," the "nations" and the "kings." This observation is particularly instructive when you recognize that the author of the prologue portrays exalted men who used to look down on the Suffering Servant when he was alive, now they are unable to get beyond their shock and grief (the great ones), as they perceived what had never been told to them and they understood what they never heard (the vast nations), and the kings adopt a posture of sulking and refuse to rejoice over the Servant. While there are key differences between the two interpretations, the key takeaway for purposes of this work is the notion that God uses the suffering and death of the Servant to show its connection to the suffering of God's people which, in turn, causes a reaction in the nations as they realize that God will ultimately exalt that which they vilified and mistreated.

When we get to the body of the section, Seitz agrees with B.S. Childs, author of *Isaiah: Old Testament Library*, noting that there is a connection between 52:15 and 53:1, stating that the "servants who are making confession regarding the work of the servant (53:1-9), begin by stating that what they have come to know was not and is not in any way obvious." As they begin their report, they question who is going to be able to understand it and openly articulate that "comprehension will require the hand of the Lord."

Michael L. Barre, author of *Textual and Rhetorical-critical Observations on the Last Servant Song*, also sees the speakers of 53:1 in the prologue, but not in (52:15) like Seitz, but in the many (great ones), of 52:14, who initially couldn't grasp the significance of God's transformative purpose embodied in the Servant's death. Now at the outset of the body of the poem, they understand, and from this point, "the speakers describe their earlier perception of the Servant." Based on the two interpretations, what I surmise is that the divine revelation God has now revealed to the servants will astound the kings and the nations, thus fulfilling the earlier prophecy of Isaiah that the Servant will be a light to the nations (49:6-7). Both biblical commentators see in 53:2 that the Servant grows up in barren conditions and as such, it contributes to the servant's unattractive appearance. However, Barre's rendering of the Hebrew is such that he translates the first part of verse two as "He grew up before *us* . . ." which is quite disparate from the usual translation of "before him." Barre gives an elaborate linguistical technicality as justification for the rendering before "us," and adds that the body of the poem is narrated from the perspective of the speakers and concerns their reaction to the Servant."

Verse three continues the description of the Servant from verse two, without naming the agents responsible for the condition of the Servant who is cut off or withdrawn from humanity. Seitz embraces the notion that the Servant was violently scapegoated, while acknowledging that this verse doesn't shed light on the culprits, while Barre seems to champion that in this stanza, there is a lack of evidence to support that those who "disesteemed the Servant treated him with hostility, let alone violence." In verse 4, the commentators seemingly arrive at the same conclusion, that a shift in understanding the nature of the suffering of the Servant has occurred. Barre observes that the great ones understand the Servant's sufferings as afflictions sent by God, whereas Seitz focuses on the meaning of the Servant's suffering: "his condition was made to serve the purpose of bearing something not naturally his alone, but rightfully accruing to others." In verse 5, Seitz focuses on the notion that the servants realize that the divine physical assault of the Servant is for the purpose of healing and reconciling them, even as they had previously considered him naturally afflicted. Barre, on the other hand, focuses on the notion that God is the agent of the Servant's suffering, like a father punishes their son. Barre emphatically argues that nothing in the first six verses "refers to any affliction of the Servant clearly brought about by human agency."

Ironically, both Seitz and Barre have little to nothing to say specifically in their respective works about verse 6. The servants continue the "we" language to characterize their behavior as sheep, certainly not a compliment. It refers to their lack of intelligence and willingness to be easily distracted and gullible to misinformation and foolish narratives. In John Gill's Exposition of the Entire Bible, in describing "we have all turned to our own way," he writes: "and that is an evil one, a dark and slippery one, a crooked one, the end of it is ruin; yet this is a way of a man's own choosing and approving, and in which he delights . . ." The last part of verse 6, where the author speaks of the Lord laying on the Servant the iniquity of us all, is for me in direct alignment with the scapegoat narrative of Leviticus 16, where the Lord taught Jews to purge the community of its iniquities by having the high priest "lay both of his hands on the live goat, and confess over it all the iniquities of the people of Israel, and all their transgressions, and all their sins, putting them on the head of the goat . . ." (Leviticus 16:21)

In verse seven, the double mention of the Servant choosing not to verbally object to the mistreatment he receives may not be considered directly in alignment with the scapegoating narrative in Leviticus since the animal is literally incapable of objecting to the mistreatment. But the sentiment of being forced to endure the suffering which unconsciously leads to their own demise is present in both narratives. Furthermore, in the scapegoat scandal of Joseph by his brothers, Joseph was "silenced," unable to escape the wrath of his brothers' iniquities and was sold as a slave to Midianites who eventually went to Egypt. Once in Egypt, Joseph has the opportunity to verbally "out" his brothers for their mistreatment, but like the Servant in Isaiah 53, he chose to be "silent," and decided not to let Jacob know what had happened. When the brothers fear Joseph seeking revenge, they scapegoat their father in order to curry mercy from Joseph. Joseph saw God's will in the process, "even though you intended to do harm to me, God intended it for good, in order to preserve a numerous people, as he is doing today" (Genesis 50:20). Both Barre and Seitz all group the last verses of the main section together in their analysis but arrive at completely different conclusions. Whereas Barre uses detailed, and some might opine, novel etymological analysis to stay consistent to his belief that God and God alone seemingly punished the Servant, and that there is no explicit statement of the death of the servant in the poem, Seitz believes that "the language of the text is clear enough: there is a grave and a death." How one interprets the beginning verses of the poem informs how one understands how the body of the poem ends. If we believe that the graphic descriptions of suffering in the poem function more in a rhetorically, metaphorical fashion, it shapes how we interpret the mentioning of a grave as more in tune with "Babylonian poems that speak of burial rites being performed for the sufferer while he is alive, and his suffering as not from the hands of human beings but as punishment from God."

On the other hand, if we allow the mistreatment of the Servant to function on a more visceral, literal plane, then we see the violent descriptions of mistreatment of the Servant in the latter half of the poem as leading to an actual death and burial for sins he did not commit. For me personally, I want to struggle to appreciate the rhetorical sentiments of the poem and the theologies of messianic prophecy and eschatology wrapped in the language of violent scapegoating. It is not an either/or but a both/and proposition. The characterizations that describe the mistreatment intensify as the poem develops. First, "we" just thought the Servant was an ungodly nobody, and that His affliction was naturally induced essentially from birth. By extension, "we" disregarded and despised him accordingly, but now realize that God ordained him to suffer because of and for our afflictions. His mistreatment became a propitiation for our own sins and as a result, "we" are beneficiaries of healing. God chose Him to be our scapegoat carrying the weight of our wickedness. Like a scapegoat, He carried it all without complaint, though the oppression and the mistreatment warranted an ear-deafening outcry at the very least. "By a perversion of justice he was taken away . . . cut off from the land of the living, stricken for the transgression of my people," (53:8) a dead, spot-on tactic straight from the playbook of scapegoating in Leviticus 16. As I intimated in the previous chapter when describing the relationship between the immolated goat offered to God and the scapegoat driven away for Azazel, even though one goat lives, in essence by being cast out away from community, that "live "goat is in effect dead. And the community responds to the goat as if it were dead precisely because of its being "stricken for the transgression of my people." The shift from second person speech to third person speech in verses 7-9 for me is also undeniably insightful; a shift almost imperceptible (up to this point we get the sense that the servants could possibly be the agents of oppression, even while it is certain that they are culpable in some form of mistreatment of the Servant despite them being beneficiaries because of His suffering). Its presence forces us to entertain the possibility that the "we" of the earlier verses which signaled the servants may now have transitioned to "they" (53:9 NRSV, ESV, HCSB), a different demographic altogether. Although the Servant is clearly depicted by the author of the poem as innocent, by the time we get to verse nine, they disregard and reject His innocence, blatantly creating the context where the Servant will be seen in a negative light (an intent which ends up utterly failing as the suffering and death end up ushering in a positive "light for the nations").

While I appreciate both approaches to this complex passage, Barre's analysis leaves me wanting, not because I am a Christian and desperately need this text to precisely mimic the death and resurrection of Jesus for it to be Messianic (its Messianic overtones run much deeper than that for me), but because of his insistence that God alone punishes the Servant, which for me can't be made to align with 53:8a, which Barre skips over in his analysis to focus on 8cd. This is tragic because 53:8a sheds valuable light in the realization that the Servant becomes a victim in a judicial process that inflicts oppression. As one commentator puts it, the Servant is taken "by a violence which cloaked itself under the formalities of a legal process."

This is instructive because the God I serve is not a God who perverts justice, because justice is Yahweh's modus operandi. Justice is one of the most significant themes of the Bible, so for Barre to advocate that no human beings were involved in the suffering of the Servant, it would mean that God singularly and intentionally put aside one of the core characteristics that differentiates God from everything and everyone else. I won't say God would never . . . but I need some pretty conclusive evidence before I am going to believe that God would hold justice hostage and purposefully design violent scapegoating of humans to be associated with God's perfect will. That evidence with regard to this verse, in particular, is lacking, and thus we must consider the probability that God took what evil meant for bad and turned it for our own good, a formula found throughout the canon.

On the other hand, when I think about Joseph in Genesis, the scapegoat in Leviticus 16, Jesus in the gospels, and the Suffering Servant here, what I can embrace is how God situates Himself in the midst of violence and reenvisions, reimagines it so that His holy will is made manifest, over and above the violence caused by humans and fueled by iniquity. For me, this common thread is glaring and strengthens my resolve that God doesn't desire for suffering yet is willing and able to reappropriate it so that it functions to purge, wipe, expiate, shed light, and atone. If in Isaiah 53, we have a poignant and powerful scene of (gross) injustice as Seitz states, then by definition, human beings and evil have come together in some insidious manner, and God being God fashions a way to transform it for redeeming purposes.

CHAPTER 4

REVELATIONS FROM THE FUNCTION OF SCAPEGOATING IN THE GOSPEL NARRATIVES

The gospel narratives contain rich soil for us to mine and examine how the scapegoating scandal and rituals we found in the Old Testament, persist and evolve in the New Testament. Most revealing is that there are essentially two main stakeholders in the gospels who use their power to weaponize scapegoating: the Jews and the Romans. When I use the phrase "the Jews," I mean to refer specifically to the Jewish elite during antiquity, not all Jews. There are a host of ways to examine scapegoating in the gospels, but I believe it fruitful to look at the gospels as they narrate the life of Jesus from infant baby through crucified Lamb of God. And to really underscore the differences both big and small between the four versions of Jesus' life, I believe it to be fruitful to analyze the synoptic gospels collectively when a scene involving scapegoating occurs in Matthew, Mark and Luke, but on the other hand, set apart John's gospel, precisely because the latter differentiates itself from the other three in terms of its form, purpose, and scope. Let's go over the background context for each of the four gospels, because recalling that critical information is especially useful in appreciating the nuances from gospel to gospel.

Matthew writes to the Jewish community for the specific purpose of showing that Jesus fulfills 57 prophecies regarding the Messiah told in the Old Testament. Though they are expecting a conquering king, the Savior enters the world as a baby boy and thus Matthew's gospel is an attempt to compel Jews to recognize through the fulfillment of Old Testament scripture, who Jesus really is. Mark's gospel opens by immediately characterizing the ministry of John the Baptist, to showcasing the baton being passed as Jesus begins where His predecessor (John the Baptist) left off. Shortly thereafter, Mark goes from one action-packed scene to the next, climaxing with chapters 6 through 16 focused on Jesus' agony, driving home the point that "Jesus, the Son of God, came to earth to take the punishment for humanity's sin by suffering and dying." Luke in his own unique way, combines elements of Matthew's beginning (the birth of Jesus) and Mark's beginning (showcasing John the Baptist). The gospel of Luke goes out of its way to portray Jesus as a compassionate lover of the demonized, the outcast, the oppressed. The Jesus of Luke's gospel comes to proclaim God's salvation for all flesh, not just for Israel alone. In John, Jesus is the very Logos or Word of God made incarnate. As Living Word, Jesus is not characterized as a victim in any way; instead, John's gospel portrays Jesus as one who intentionally puts himself in harm's way as a means of revealing his Messiahship.

King Herod Scapegoats the Male Babies in Bethlehem

It is tempting to go straight to the passion of Christ to examine the nature of scapegoating in the gospels, but if we are honest with ourselves, scapegoating in the New Testament starts at the very beginning of the life of Jesus. Obery Hendricks in his landmark publication, *The Politics of Jesus*, does a masterful job of pointing out the normative function of scapegoating during Jesus' time without calling it scapegoating when he chronicles the slaughter at Sepphoris right around the time of Jesus' birth, and masterfully connects it to the violent sentiments surrounding "the horrific victimization of Emmett Till." However, in looking at the political machinations surrounding the birth of Jesus, the gospel of Matthew exclusively showcases scapegoating on an epic scale just after baby Jesus was born.

In chapter two, magi from the East travel to Jerusalem, and upon arrival, they ask, "Where is the child who is born King of the Jews?" The question intimidates the then Roman king of the Jews, King Herod, who upon hearing of the magi and their question, asks his chief scribes and priests where the Messiah is to be born. They quote Old Testament prophecy and tell King Herod the Messiah is to be born in Bethlehem, who then relays the location of the newborn king to the magi, and he requests that the magi get word of the location back to the king, so that he may "pay homage" too. After the magi locate Jesus and pay homage, God causes the magi to dream that they are not to go back and tell King Herod the newborn king's location. When Herod eventually realizes that the magi have tricked him, his fear/anger drives him to kill all the male boys in and around Bethlehem who were two years old and under. Thus we have an act of horrendous violence, targeting a specific group of boys according to their location, an act that in every other instance would be considered heinous, but because it will neutralize a formidable threat, the scapegoating is made justifiable. The gross ungodliness of the king's use of scapegoating is made clear in the observation that the king sacrifices the innocent lives of hundreds if not thousands of children, whereas the mere killing of one goat in Leviticus 16 atones/appeases for the defilement caused by the sins of hundreds if not thousands of Jews. The comparison of the mentality of scapegoating between the two narratives is the same (in terms of neutralizing a threat on behalf of the community); yet the contrast between the scope of scapegoating in Matthew chapter two versus Leviticus 16 couldn't be starker.

Using Sabbath Violations to Justify Criminalizing Jesus

Unlike the exclusive Matthean narrative of King Herod destroying an army of male babies under two years old in the vicinity of Bethlehem, the narratives of Jesus healing on the Sabbath which ultimately incite the Jewish leadership to want to violently harm Him is in all four gospels. In each of the synoptic gospels (Matthew 12:9-14, Mark 3:1-6, and Luke 6:6-11), when Jesus heals the man with the withered hand, the Jewish authorities in the three accounts detail how they reacted and noted them conspiring to kill/destroy Jesus. The shift to examine scapegoating on the Sabbath after looking at King Herod's scapegoating of the male babies of Bethlehem, stems from its early occurrence in Mark's gospel, not because I believe that it is the next occurrence of collective scapegoating as told in the gospels. The lack of chronological narration and the real differences between the authors' recalling of the narratives makes ascertaining a bona fide chronological sequencing difficult.

Not only is understanding the sequence of collective scapegoating during the life of Jesus difficult to nail down in the gospels, but there is also great nuance between the gospels in terms of how violating the Sabbath law turned into a justification to scapegoat. At first glance, one can discover the popular narrative of the healing of the man with the withered hand in the synagogue on the Sabbath being absent exclusively in John's gospel. There is not much difference between the synoptics regarding Jesus healing the man with the withered hand, as each of the non-Johnian accounts takes note of the reaction of the Jewish leaders who want to destroy Jesus. However, while we could examine the dynamics of scapegoating as it relates specifically to the narration of the withered hand, the gospel of Luke in its account, exclusively portrayed Jesus being scapegoated. While the withered hand scene is told in Luke 6, it is in Luke chapter 4, where Jesus has defeated the devil in the wilderness, that shortly thereafter, Jesus went into the synagogue (on the Sabbath). And after saying a few words, Luke's gospel reports that all who were in the synagogue, when they heard these things, "They got up, drove him out of the town, and led him to the brow of the hill on which their town was built, so that they might hurl him off the cliff. But he passed through the midst of them and went on his way" (Luke 4:29-30). What is it that Jesus says, that enrages the Jews to want to violently kill Him? In verse 22 of chapter four, "they all spoke well of him and were amazed at the gracious words that came from his mouth," but by verse 28, they had transitioned from being amazed by Jesus to being incensed by Him. His recalling of Isaiah's prophecy didn't ruffle their feathers despite its clear messaging of God instituting a new season of justice and liberation that will empower those who were powerless. But in verses 25-27, when He expounds upon the recipients of God's promise and it becomes clear to them that the blessing of God's anointing would not be on them, but instead would cross ethnic boundaries, liberate the oppressed and upend the status quo, the joy of the Jews quickly turned into outrage.

When Jesus recalls the history of Elijah and Elisha, He draws upon a legacy of God's anointed prophets purposefully skipping over some Israelites to bless Gentiles. In recalling this history, Jesus is identifying His ministry with their legacy of being intentionally inclusive. The scandal of scapegoating almost always occurs when perceived privilege is idolized and efforts to redistribute power and create a more equitable means of sharing resources are seen as a threat to that power. With Joseph and his brothers in Genesis, they saw Joseph's privilege accessed by the favoritism of their father Jacob as a threat to their desire for Jacob to treat the brothers equitably. In Luke, when the Jews see Jesus aligning His ministry with the prophets Elijah and Elisha, who empowered Gentiles, the same threat to power that Joseph's brothers had consumed their persona, and the same rationale for succumbing to the seduction of scapegoating, which ultimately leads to violence raised its ugly head. What is so absurd about this on a metaphysical level is that it is not as if God cannot bless Gentiles and run out of "blessing" or "favor" for Jews. With humans, material resources can run out, and when real-world assets become scarce, it is harder to resist becoming self-centered. But in the spiritual realm, God's omniscience and omnipotence translate into an ability and willingness to bestow compassion in ways that break down social and cultural barriers. Bible scholar R. Alan Culpepper puts it this way, "Throughout history the gospel has always been more radically inclusive than any group, denomination, or church, so we continually struggle for a breadth of love and acceptance that more nearly approximates the breadth of God's love." Jesus' modus operandi is not governed by loyalty to a preferred subset who have been previously identified as God's chosen. Because Jesus shuns hierarchy and instead operates from the power of the Holy Spirit, the Jews see their privileged status as moot in Jesus' ministry. As men and women of faith, we must personify community in ways that exemplify that our cup runs over, and that we are immune to feeling threatened when God decides to bless those who don't identify with folks in our inner circles. True followers of Jesus not only shun feeling threatened by God blessing others, but we rejoice when God bestows blessings on others believing that what the Lord has done for others, God will do for us.

Having discussed how Jesus' teaching ministry in Luke's gospel begins in the temple on the Sabbath, first triggering astonishment which ultimately gave way to enragement, now let us look at the other activities Jesus did on the Sabbath, which triggered the Jews' fury such that they were prone to become violent. There are two other actions that the gospels record Jesus doing on the Sabbath that provoke a violent response from the Jews and both involve healing. As mentioned before, the synoptics recount Jesus healing the man with the withered hand on the Sabbath, and the gospel of John recounts Jesus healing the man waiting at the pool of Bethesda with a 38-year-old infirmity. I will turn back to the accounts regarding healing the withered hand on the Sabbath, then focus on the healing of the man by the Bethesda pool last. While there are enticing, exegetical nuances that exist between the three synoptic accounts featuring the healing of the man with the withered hand, I do not believe those nuances to be relevant to our discussion about scapegoating here. What is relevant is that in all three accounts the gospel writers specifically point out that the scribes and the Pharisees are measuring Jesus to see if He would cure the man on the Sabbath. Having perused the perspectives of several biblical experts, I am mindful not to minimize the importance of Sabbath observance, nor do I ignore the possibility that in some Jewish communities, there may have been some debate about whether it was appropriate to conduct a non-life-threatening healing on the Sabbath. It is important to highlight that the Jewish faith is hardly monolithic, just as the Christian faith is not either. Despite the significant differences between the context of the different gospel traditions, it seems significant that they all share the notion that clearly, hostility towards Jesus had already baked in. And rather than objectively allowing the nature of the actions unfolding to inform their perspective, the scriptures allow us to see that the scribes and the Pharisees are eager to trap Jesus. One of the hallmark actions associated with scandalous scapegoating is the enthusiasm/premeditation to demonize or criminalize. This nefarious agenda begins to bubble over when Jesus' disciples plucked grain in the field on a Sabbath, and to really appreciate the forces at work concerning the man with the withered hand in the synagogue, it is instructive to look at this prior conflict on the Sabbath between Jesus and the Pharisees. Just as Joseph was seen as a threat to his brothers, when Jesus verbally outwits the Pharisees in defending the actions of the disciples, and proclaimed Himself Lord of the Sabbath, they began to see Him as a threat. Not only had Jesus verbally outsmarted the Pharisees, but He also exposed them for who they were. In their objection to both taking and eating grain and healing the withered hand on the Sabbath, the Pharisees weaponized the Law to subvert one of the essential

Jewish tenets of the Sabbath, the disposition of mercy, especially toward the poor and hungry. In this case, the disciples, having left all, were both poor and hungry, and the man with the withered hand, not being able to work, was in all likelihood poor.

Having thus been exposed by Jesus in the grainfields on the Sabbath, the scribes and Pharisees go into the synagogue eager to accuse Jesus of violating the Sabbath, when they themselves, in their wicked, violent scheming *in the synagogue,* are unashamedly violating the Sabbath. While the gospel accounts of the healing of the withered hand on the Sabbath share many elements, I do believe it would be a mistake to gloss over how Mark's gospel exclusively has Jesus drawing the Pharisees into direct confrontation with Him when He asks the man to come forward and then challenges them by asking "Is it lawful to do good or to do harm on the Sabbath, to save life or to kill?" In one swipe, Jesus in the gospel of Mark (and not in Matthew or Luke) was exposing His agenda to honor the Sabbath by doing good and saving a life while simultaneously uncovering the religious leaders' agenda to do harm on the Sabbath and kill (Mark 3:6). My brother and colleague who I hold in high regard, Obery Hendricks, has stated that the anger "Jesus displays in the gospels is never because of his own mistreatment, but is his response to the oppression and mistreatment of others." In chapter two, Mark had already shared with his readers how Jesus is able to discern the hidden conspiring of the people, and here in chapter three, the silence of the leaders to his question exposes their plot. Therefore, I respectfully disagree with my colleague and cannot see Jesus being fully human without embodying an anger towards the hardened hearts of the religious leaders not only because of their oppressive interpretation of the law and its victimization upon God's people, but also because of the Pharisees' eagerness to weaponize the Law to "cover" their own ungodly desire to kill (scapegoat) Him. In other words, the Pharisees use God's Word on the Sabbath to violate the Word (both written and personified in Jesus).

Finally, let us turn to the notion of Jesus healing the paralytic man by the Bethesda pool on the Sabbath. This narrative is unlike the Markan Sabbath story, in that the Jews were not intently looking to trap Jesus to see if He would break the Sabbath; they had been triggered by seeing the paralytic man healed and carrying his mat, so they called him out on carrying his mat. It is only when the healed man describes that "the man who made me well said to me, 'Take up your mat and walk,'" that the Jews turn their attention to the one who ordered the man to violate the Sabbath. John's gospel is written in such a way that the confrontation between earthly authority and God's authority is front and center. In fact, a confrontation between the authorities has already happened in John's gospel prior to chapter five when Jesus drives out the moneychangers from the temple in chapter two. Ironically, the confrontation of Jesus cleansing the temple in John's gospel doesn't end with the Jews desiring to scapegoat Jesus, which supports skipping over John's narrative in chapter two and going straight to the first uncovering of a premeditated desire to murder Jesus in John chapter five. Despite the lack of an aggressive response by the Jews to the confrontation in chapter two, when viewing it there along with the confrontation here, John paints the picture of Jesus being deliberate in creating confrontation. His actions against the moneychangers provoke a response, albeit a nonviolent one and His actions here in chapter five provoke a response, this time, one that triggers a series of events that ultimately lead to His unjust execution. Gail R. O' Day in her commentary on the gospel of John points out that Jesus' provoking in chapter 5 begins when He tells the paralytic to rise, take up his mat and walk, and those same three commands are in Mark 2:9. While the three commands along with the healing miracle in Mark are situated in a house, on a non-Sabbath day, among a cloud of witnesses including scribes, the same three words in John trigger quite a different response when spoken by the pool, on the Sabbath, and initially, no one knew who had healed the paralytic. But the anonymity Jesus enjoyed in John's gospel is short-lived as his narrative has Jesus revisiting the healed man later the same day in the synagogue, and the story is structured to let us know that this reconnection is specifically to empower the man to be able to go back to the Jews (who have in the interim asked) and tell them who healed him.

Once the identity of the man who told the paralytic to pick up his mat and walk was revealed, a series of conversations ensued on two themes; one on the man being made well, contrasted with picking up the mat being constituted as a Sabbath violation. As mentioned previously, I am not trying to minimize the nature of Sabbath violation being a big deal for Jews during the time of Jesus. But on another level, I am struck by the irony that making a man well would violate the Sabbath. If praying and worshipping God and going to the temple are acceptable activities on the Sabbath, I am at a loss as to how providing healing violates the spirit of the Sabbath. This alone ought to cause us to be suspicious of the true agenda of these Jewish leaders who reject Jesus. When you add to the objection of Sabbath violation, the observation of their preoccupation with identifying the one who told the healed man to take up his mat, once revealed, they singularly focused on Jesus. They operated as if the man carrying the mat, which initially triggered them, was innocent. This laser-precision focus on persecuting Jesus, and the overlooking of holding accountable all involved in the "Sabbath violation" speaks volumes. There has been much discussion from scholars as to the intent of the healed man initially disclosing to the Jews that his healer commanded that he arise, take up his mat, and walk. More relevant for this book, is, what is the intent of the Jewish elite, and I believe their fixation on Jesus sheds valuable light in that regard. They wanted to confront the one who incited the Sabbath violation so much so that they were willing to exonerate the paralytic. The healed man had options, one of which was to arise and not take up the mat and walk; but he chose to break the letter of the law of the Sabbath, yet the Jews totally gloss over that to focus on Jesus. I am not advocating that the healed man should be punished for his Sabbath violation; I'm just pointing out the inconsistency in applying the principle across the board and how that inconsistency reveals intent. As we shall see in later narratives of scapegoating in the New Testament, this selective application of ignoring some to target others is a reoccurring feature of scandalous scapegoating. When seen through this lens, violation of the Law is hardly the focus, the issue is power and the obsession of making sure that no one but the Jewish leaders are permitted to define how life is ordered, how religion is practiced and is present in the world. Jesus' pushback on the absurdity of their calling out of a Sabbath violation, and His framing of God as His Father, is just the ammunition the Jews need to tap into their insidious conspiring. The gravity of the threat by Jesus fuels the violent backlash of a religious leadership hell-bent on doing whatever it takes to destroy the threat to their power. This is the bedrock upon which scandalous scapegoating thrusts itself into being . . . the audacity to want to use God's Word, in the synagogue, to justify murdering a healer who made a man well on the Sabbath.

The other major difference between the synoptics version of this healing versus John's gospel version is that in John's gospel, the Pharisees began to persecute Jesus immediately after the healed man told them that it was Jesus who healed him. John lets us know that after disclosing to the Pharisees who Jesus is, the healed man went away to emphasize this showdown between Jesus and the Pharisees in the synagogue on the Sabbath. In the synoptics, Jesus performed many healings and expressly told the one healed not to tell anyone (Matthew 8:4, 12:16, Mark 1:44, 3:12, 5:43, 7:36, 8:26, Luke 5:14, 8:56). But in John's gospel, Jesus never conceals His identity, which speaks to the notion that one of the purposes of John's gospel is to reveal that Jesus is the Messiah. Furthermore, John orchestrates this healing narrative particularly to show Jesus making sure that the healed man is able to identify and reveal to the Pharisees who healed him, and then has Jesus remain in the synagogue to confront the Pharisees' persecution of Him for His Sabbath violation. Conversely, in the synoptics, the Sabbath violation by Jesus shows no direct verbal confrontation, but has the Pharisees going away scheming to kill Jesus. John's gospel has no interest in concealing the identity of Jesus, and by having the cleansing of the temple near the outset of Jesus' ministry (compared to the cleansing of the temple narrative being situated near the close of Jesus' ministry in the synoptics), John's gospel both in chapter two and here in chapter five, demonstrate Jesus reclaiming the temple to be under God's authority, usurping the temple authority of the religious leaders, which triggers them to rebel. The temple leaders have had no problem operating in ways to use the temple to oppress the masses, even on the Sabbath, so Jesus' statement about working because "My Father is still working," is cover for the Pharisees to justify their pseudo-righteous indignation against Jesus. They wanted the ability to operate as they have done on the Sabbath (shutting down all work had crushed the poor yet posed few problems for the well-heeled) but couldn't allow anybody else to enjoy the same privilege.

For me the eagerness of the religious leaders to characterize Jesus as a violator of the Sabbath indicates premeditation, especially in the synoptic narratives, to use Sabbath violation as a way to criminalize Jesus. The opportunity to characterize Jesus as one who broke the law becomes the justification for mistreatment and victimization via scapegoating. As I stated above, in John's gospel, it is less clear that there was premeditation when the Pharisees first encountered the healed man carrying his mat, on the Sabbath, in the synagogue, but once they interrogate the healed man, their preoccupation with the healer (and ignoring the one healed) who commands the healed to take up his mat on the Sabbath, reveals a propensity to criminalize Jesus. Scholars have intimated about the controversy during Jesus' time regarding whether nonessential healings on the Sabbath were legal/appropriate. In other words, it wasn't a black or white issue. Yet these passages show leaders who saw Jesus as a threat, and they used Sabbath violation as a tool to scapegoat.

Demonization Used as a Tool to Scapegoat

One of the purposes of chronicling scandalous scapegoating in the gospel narratives is to see if patterns emerge that will help identify, dissect, and ultimately mitigate its harmful effects. Characterizing someone as a criminal is a hallmark strategy focused on interpreting behavior as a threat and thus using that characterization to justify violence. While I have focused on passages where the threat of physical violence is clear, even if occasionally veiled, I do think we can gain insights about scandalous scapegoating from violent language too. The language of the religious leaders not only reveals their willingness to use criminalization to scapegoat but demonization as well. The passages of scripture where Jesus is accused of being demon-possessed along with the exorcism of the demon(s) of Gerasa showcase how demonizing, violence and scapegoating feed off each other in subtle and overt ways.

I assert that calling someone demon-possessed is an act of violence in and of itself, because it stigmatizes the individual from a labeling perspective, opening them up to ostracizing, alienation, and ridicule. It is also an act of violence because it allows stakeholders to use the person's demon possession to be violent towards them since they can claim that the unpredictability and unstableness of the individual caused them to fear for their life.

The call of Jesus being demon-possessed occurs in the synoptic gospels at Mark 3:20-30, Matthew 12:22-32, and Luke 11:14-23. Since the consensus by scholars is that Mark is the oldest of the three, and that Matthew and Luke both have material borrowed from Mark's gospel, it is ironic to see that only in Mark's gospel, the labeling by Jesus' family as Him being "out of His mind," feeding (i.e., setting up) the call of the Pharisees to label Him as operating under the ruler of demons, Beelzebul. Why Matthew and Luke (purposefully) choose to exorcise this portion of the pericope is fascinating albeit challenging to definitively pinpoint. The mischaracterization of those closest to Jesus sets the stage for enemies of Jesus to intentionally malign Jesus as a pretext for scapegoating Him. As Pheme Hawkins points out in her New Interpreters' Bible Commentary on Mark, when two episodes in Mark are intertwined, they illuminate each other. The violence of his family toward him, bolstered by the labeling of Jesus as out of his mind, seduces them into believing it was appropriate to physically restrain him. The enemies of Jesus use the same formula, verbally calling Him demon-possessed, and using the false accusation as a means to charge Jesus with an act that justifies using physical violence to subdue Him. In this way, Mark's gospel here in chapter three verse 21, illuminates how demonization and criminalization intertwine to scapegoat Jesus. I will come back to this compelling dialectic later. What is revelatory for me about the scene is that in all three gospels, albeit not in identical ways, Jesus demonstrates the power of being possessed by the Holy Spirit, which the demons in others properly recognize, yet His own family and the religious leaders, while accusing Jesus, accuse Him of being out of His mind or demon-possessed, when they are themselves possessed by the demon of willful unbelief. Reflecting thoughtfully on the function of scapegoating in accusing Jesus of being demon-possessed, I am reminded of how some police officers are hypervigilant in identifying criminality in others—as if it is the tool of choice to keep the spotlight off of their own criminality vis-a-vis racial profiling, excessive force, and other scapegoat tactics that support upholding white supremacy. And I am also reminded of the demonizing language presidential candidate Trump used to characterize immigrants, Mexicans, BLM protestors, women and others, which branded him as the political contender most willing to tap into the white fear of losing their privileged status as we inch closer to whites becoming a majority minority in less than three decades. His ability to ride that strategy to victory in 2016, seduced him into continuing to utilize demonizing language to scapegoat anyone who pushed back on his agenda to operate in the Office of the President as an autocrat. He demonized my elementary school classmate, White House reporter April Ryan because of her courage to ask tough questions. And in remarks to law enforcement officers in Brentwood, NY in July of 2017, President Trump demonized gang members who commit violence, calling them animals and encouraged officers to "not be too nice" in the process of arresting them. Demonizing became one of Trump's signature tools throughout his Administration to justify violent scapegoating.

The narrative of the Gerasene demoniac, found in all three synoptic gospels, is rich in helping us tease out how scandalous scapegoating fuels communal violence. Of the three descriptions of the background information that helps frame the scene, Mark's and Luke's gospels both state that the demon-possessed man from the town lived in the tombs. One of the ways demonology functions is by playing into the notion that you can judge someone based on where they live. Those who live in more affluent locales are not characterized despairingly, while those who live in squalor, abject poverty, or crime-infested neighborhoods are often the targets of demonization. Trump personified this practice of demonizing when he asked, "Why America would want immigrants from 'all these shithole countries' and that the U.S. should have more people coming in from places like Norway," during a meeting on January 11, 2018, with a bipartisan group of senators at the White House regarding his frustration with the visa lottery immigration system.

And yet, Mark's narrative is unique in going further to paint the picture of the demon-possessed man from Gerasa who is living in the tombs. In verse three of chapter five, Mark states that "no one could restrain him anymore, even with a chain; for he had often been restrained with shackles and chains, but the chains he wrenched apart, and the shackles he broke into pieces; and no one had the strength to subdue him."

Having been forever affected by watching the concrete lynching of George Floyd, that event and God's inspiration have transformed how I see this scripture, so much so that I preached a two-part sermon series in October of 2020, entitled "When Life Drives Us Crazy" Parts One and Two. In Part One I mentioned that despite the lack of specificity in the Gerasene demoniac passage as to how the man became demon-possessed, his extended dwelling among the tombs enabled and exacerbated his mental condition. I drew parallels to how too many black and brown people are suffering mentally because we have been manipulated to dwell in the midst of so much death.

In Part 2 of the two-part sermon series "When Life Drives Us Crazy," I highlighted the incredible dichotomy of the failed attempts to directly bind and restrict the demon-possessed man with chains, that he repeatedly broke, and juxtaposed it with his chronic inability to divorce himself from living in the tombs. No matter the chains used, he was able to break loose from them, but no matter the moment of breaking out, it never translated into transformation. At the end of the day, he still found himself bound to a life among tombs. The visible chains the scapegoaters used could be overcome, but the invisible chains kept him mentally unhinged and living in the tombs, which he could not break out of on his own.

The people of the town had no problem with this dysfunctional cycle, which is evidenced by their repetitive use of physical chains that the demon-possessed man could defeat. If they were serious about punishing him for breaking the chains, they could've escalated the type of bondage they utilized and eventually found a more secure way of bondage that he couldn't overcome. Instead, they continued to use chains he could break out of . . . because they knew that the invisible mental chains in his head kept him imprisoned in the tombs.

The Beheading of John the Baptist

Earlier, we identified the origin of scandalous scapegoating by referring to the dysfunctional dynamic between Joseph and his brothers in Genesis 37-42. Now we have two New Testament brothers, both called Herod, whose dysfunctional relationship results in communal violence. One brother is Herod Antipas, tetrarch of Galilee and Perea, and ruler throughout Jesus of Nazareth's ministry. The other is Herod Philip I, half-brother of Herod Antipas. Both shared the same father Herod the Great, but Herod Philip I's mother was Marianne II, while Herod Antipas' mother was Malthace. All in all, Herod the Great had 10 wives and so the incestuous dysfunction is hardly limited to the sibling rivalry between Herod Antipas and Herod

Philip I. As biblical scholars note, the dynamic between Herod Antipas, his (second) wife Herodias, and John the Baptist, mirrors the dynamic between Ahab, Jezebel and Elijah in 1 Kings 17-19. In each of these narratives, a ruler over God's people is influenced by his wife to go against the word of the prophet. Furthermore, the stories are connected because the women in power use their influence to facilitate a plot to violently scapegoat the prophet of God, who calls out the wrongdoing of the ruler/king and their wives by extension. In addition, the context around the beheading of John the Baptist, principally the overtly incestuous nature of the family dynamics of Herod the Great's offspring, wreaks of privilege prone to violently react to any threat to its power.

It is here that I draw from the compelling insights of one Rene Girard, often called the father of the scapegoat mechanism. Girard has a foundational concept in scapegoating called mimetic desire. In mimesis, two people want the same thing, one imitating the other's desires, and they consciously or unconsciously compete to possess the object desired. The nature of rivalry fuels the justification of scapegoating, which often turns violent. In his landmark book called *The Scapegoat*, Girard dedicated chapter 11 to unfolding the insidious, competing desires embedded in the context of the beheading of John the Baptist. Family rivalry is woven into the very fabric of the context of the narrative as Herod Antipas divorces his first wife to marry Herodias, who had been married to Herod Antipas' half-brother Herod Philip I. Girard characterizes John the Baptist's rebuke of Herod Antipas' possessing of Herodias as "warning his royal listener against the evil effects of mimetic desire." Antipas throws John the Baptist in jail, but as Girard points out, his unwillingness to kill John the Baptist at her bidding infuriates her. Here then is mimetic desire ultimately triggering violence. Herodias cannot bear being humiliated by the prophet and being denied by her husband, which she interpreted, gave credibility to the prophet's claims, so she exploits her privilege as a member of the royal family to justify her rage to murder the prophet by any means necessary. If it means using her daughter Salome from her first marriage to entice her own husband Antipas, then so be it. Antipas does not want to fulfill Salome's request to have John the Baptist's head on a platter, but having promised to give Salome whatever she wants, Antipas is forced to comply or risk losing his credibility as a ruler. In this sense, the beheading, orchestrated by Herodias convincing Salome to demand the beheading, is not just the fulfilling of a request, it becomes a violent murder conducted by the ruling family (government), sanctioned by the community. As the scapegoat mechanism unfolds, it reveals rivalries on multiple levels; the two Herods (Antipas versus Philip I), Herodias versus Herod Antipas, Salome versus Herodias, and Antipas versus Salome.

The grotesque abuse of power by Herodias is a dynamic that has been exploited by women of privilege for centuries as they enthusiastically scapegoat anyone who challenges their entitlement. While many examples in history personify the same dynamics of privilege at play, since this work was instigated by the violent scapegoating of George Floyd on May 25, 2020, I couldn't dare overlook the irony that on the very same day, another case of scapegoating took place that fortunately didn't result in violence, although I am certain it was the intent.

Embodying the role of John the Baptist, Christian Cooper was bird-watching in The Ramble, a wooded area of Central Park in New York City, when he noticed and called out one Amy Cooper, who was violating Central Park regulations that restrict dog walkers to keep their dog on a leash in that particular section of the park designated for bird-watching. Amy Cooper, playing the role of Herodias, was so incensed (Mark 6:19) that a black man would attempt to hold her accountable, that she manufactured a lie, to justify calling 911, falsely asserting that Christian Cooper had assaulted her and that he had threatened her, with the hope that the police (unwittingly playing the part of Herod Antipas) would violate the scapegoat (via an unjustified arrest at the very least). Fortunately, the gospel narrative of Herodias being denied by Herod Antipas is resurrected in Central Park as the police chose not to grant Amy Cooper her wish. The same sense of entitlement Herodias embodies is evident in the actions of Amy Cooper. While Herodias' privilege stems from the lie that as a member of the Herodian dynasty, she is above reproach and thus is justified in scapegoating John the Baptist who attempted to expose her, Amy Cooper operates from a sense of entitlement that is repulsed by the notion of a black man holding her accountable and uses that as justification to scapegoat Christian Cooper.

As much as it is easy to point the finger at Herodias for setting the trap that ultimately gets Herod Antipas to facilitate the violent scapegoating of

John the Baptist, we cannot overlook his own culpability in the murder of the messenger of God. We cannot even give him a pass for initially rebuffing Herodias' initial request to kill John the Baptist. Mark 6:20 goes so far to say that Herod Antipas feared John, knowing that he was a righteous and holy man, and he protected him. When he heard him, he was greatly perplexed, and yet he liked to listen to him. Later on, we will uncover another narrative eerily similar to this one where the Son of God collides with a government ruler, who rightly perceives that the one being criminalized is righteous and thus the government ruler tries to protect the Son of God, but like Herod Antipas ultimately fails. Just in the same way Pontius Pilate doesn't get a pass despite his recognition of who Jesus is, despite his effort to avoid being a willful participant in Jesus' execution, we must not neglect to hold Herod Antipas accountable for the exact same dynamics at play in his dealings with John the Baptist. And as is my custom to apply the lens of scripture to our 21st-century context, we must hold accountable all stakeholders in positions of authority within the criminal justice system who directly or indirectly engage in promoting policies or executing procedures that violently scapegoat black and brown people. We must also eradicate the perpetuation of a culture where the entitled feel emboldened to weaponize our criminal justice system against those who have exposed or called out the ways in which members of the entitled class enjoy privileges and benefits that those non-entitled do not.

A Criminal Justice System Scapegoats the Son of God

From the arrest of Jesus by the armed mob, through the rigged trial of the Sanhedrin, to the inescapable condemning and sentencing of Jesus by Pontius Pilate, despite Pilate discerning Jesus' innocence upon interrogation, violence marks a coordinated criminal justice apparatus unable to exonerate a man conspired upon and targeted because he was a threat to exposing the oppressive economic system upon which both the Jewish religious aristocracy and the Roman government profited. Question: do the financial pressures and incentives of capitalism continue to feed into the demonization and criminalization (via mass incarceration) of black and brown bodies today through the justification and sustainment of the prison industrial complex? Absolutely!

All four of the gospel accounts have Judas and the armed mob greeting Jesus and the disciples to arrest him (Matt. 26:51-52, Mark 14:43-52, Luke 22:50, and John 18:10-11). From the lens of a scapegoat hermeneutic, the betrayal of Jesus by Judas hearkens back to Joseph's brothers betraying him in Genesis chapters 37-42. While the two are not related by blood, Judas was a disciple of Jesus, and as such, he inherited a closeness to Jesus that other followers did not enjoy. But his proximity cannot be mistaken for intimacy as his willingness to use a kiss, which normally is used to indicate compassion, as a weapon to mark Jesus, uncovers Judas' subversive agenda and as Rene Girard would say, his mimetic desire.

The nature of the elements of the event; the betrayal of Judas, the audacity of the religious officials to confront Jesus as a fortified informal militia, combined with the reality that the criminalization of an innocent Jesus was born out of a need to neutralize a threat, all work together to trigger violence. The violence that occurs during Jesus' arrest in the synoptic gospels is triggered by representatives from the mob laying their hands and apprehending the one whom the disciples had come to believe was the Messiah. In the gospel of John, the writer portrays Jesus as voluntarily surrendering himself to authorities, who are initially fearful of arresting Him. In typical Johannian fashion, Jesus is the lead actor, and the director of the scene, with the detachment of soldiers and police cowering to Jesus' power, and hesitant to walk in their "authority" despite Jesus giving them permission. Once the writer makes clear that despite Jesus allowing the armed mob to arrest Him, they are to "let these men go," the instruction of Jesus fulfills scripture by echoing John 10:29.

In Matthew, the writer only tells us that the one who violently assaults by cutting off the ear of the high priest's servant is "one of those with Jesus." In Mark, all we know is the physical attack was perpetrated by "one of those who stood near," introducing the possibility that the assailant could have been someone not directly associated with Jesus. When you combine this notion, along with the writer never mentioning Jesus restoring the servant's ear in the Markan account, it bolsters the possibility. In Luke, the writer is equally ambiguous in identifying who assaulted Caiaphas' servant, using the non-descript phrase, "one of them." Discerning the context of

Luke 22:50-52 gives credence to the probability that the writer believes the violent assaulter came from Jesus' camp based on Jesus' words "no more of this!" Furthermore, Jesus' immediate actions afterward (after restoring the ear of the slave, He addresses the mob in a way that creates separation between the indiscriminate audience first addressed right after the assault, compared to the specified audience addressed post ear restoration). Unlike the synoptic gospels, the narrative in the gospel of John is most definitive, specifically naming Simon Peter as the culprit of the assault. Highlighting the variance of the source of violence during the arrest is instructive as it prefigures the controversy in pinning down the initiator of violence when the police have disproportionately arrested black and brown bodies for suspected criminal activity. Again, I am reminded of how the Word of God, written thousands of years ago, connects with the myriad of peaceful protestors initiated because of the murder of black and brown bodies by police, being confronted by militarized police forces and the collision of the two triggering violent outbursts. While there is an assumption often made that the one being scapegoated is at fault, as is reflective of the scapegoaters in Holy Scripture, often discovering the truth is not so cut and dry.

What is most startling about the scene surrounding the arrest of Jesus is that while there is variance between the four gospels on key details, one detail is the same in all four and it has to do with what didn't happen as opposed to what should or could have happened. In none of the gospels, the culprit who violently assaults Caiaphas' servant by cutting off his ear is ever recorded as being held accountable. Such an egregious offense, one would think, would have triggered some kind of response from enforcers of the law who were there at the scene and quite possibly eyewitnesses. Why is the perpetrator not arrested? None of the gospels convey any action taken against the violent offender. I speculated that it is possible the writers thought that his arrest was not important to the story, but in light of mentioning the vicious strike of cutting off the ear of the high priest's servant, that line of reasoning fails in my opinion. If an arrest of whoever, did happen, I am confident that at least one of the writers would have mentioned it. Before George Floyd, I have perused this scene countless times and thought nothing of it. But now, I am convinced more than ever, that the lack of accountability by the angry mob, including Roman officials, is significant. What I see here is what some might characterize as selective policing. As stated on ACLU's website under police practices: "The selective policing and prosecution of low-level offenses in communities of color has led to huge racial disparities in our criminal justice system – from who is stopped, to who is charged with a crime, to who ends up under correctional control." The frenzied mob who came to arrest Jesus, who has not committed any criminal offense, is fixated on its target. They have zeroed in on scapegoating Jesus, who again they saw as a threat, and they are willing to ignore addressing a vicious assault that occurs in the midst of the arrest, because they are obsessed with capturing Jesus, who they have in their crosshairs.

What happens after the arrest varies depending on the gospel version. In Matthew, Mark and John, Jesus is sent to the high priest, with the writer of John's gospel having Him stop first to see the high priest's father-in-law Annas, who Bible scholar Raymond Brown believes embodies the role of an interrogator. Annas questions Jesus, who afterwards is on trial before the Sanhedrin with Caiaphas the high priest as its chair. Matthew and Mark's gospels are quite similar in that once Jesus is arrested; He is taken directly to the Sanhedrin to be prosecuted. Luke's gospel is most unique in that before Jesus appears before the Sanhedrin, "the men who were holding Jesus began mocking and beating him" (Luke 22:63). The scapegoating that begins with the arrest of Jesus escalates to inhuman humiliation and physical tormenting for one who has not been found guilty much less convicted of anything. In the midst of the mocking and taunting, the writer of Luke's gospel deprives Jesus of His voice. The coordination of a criminal justice system that treats you as if you are guilty long before ever proving it in court drives to the very heart of why I wrote this book. The ties between the mistreatment of black and brown bodies today and the criminalization and demonization of Jesus in the Bible for me are undeniable. They are tied together with cords that cannot be broken, no matter who tries to explain it away, justify it or whatever.

When Jesus faces the Sanhedrin, the scapegoating persists. In Matthew and Mark, it is clear that the Jewish leaders and elders of the council have already convicted and condemned Jesus and are only looking for a justification. This is textbook scapegoating; a predetermination of guilt is presumed and a strategy to manufacture or manipulate the elements so that they fit the prescribed narrative is conflated with truth or facts. Matthew's narrative goes out of its way to expose the ruse, a fixed verdict from the Sanhedrin, embellishing Mark's narrative by adding the word false before testimony. In Luke's version of the trial/hearing, the scribes, elders and chief priests are not stated as looking for testimony against Jesus because throughout Luke's gospel, the coalition has been looking for a minute for a way to get rid of Jesus (19:47, 20:19; 22:2). The equivocal response Jesus gives ("You say that I am") to the question, "Are you the Son of God?" fails to directly answer the question. But the council, having already decided Jesus' fate, use His response to justify their scapegoating, despite the lack of a definitive confession. In John's gospel, the interrogation by Annas features the physical torment by the police, while Annas is conducting his inquisition, as opposed to Luke's version, which has the tormenting executed by several people prior to the Sanhedrin trial.

The trial of Pontius Pilate versus Jesus marks the zenith of communal scapegoating in the gospels, and a number of scholars have contributed insightful analysis from that hermeneutic. Much of the analysis of this important narrative will center around the work of Jennifer K. Berenson Maclean in her article *Barabbas, the Scapegoat Ritual, and the Development of the Passion Narrative*, published in the Harvard Theological Review in 2007. I single her out because of her willingness to critique all of the major theological interpretive stances regarding the dynamic of comparing Jesus and Barabbas to the two goats in Leviticus 16; the immolated goat and the scapegoat. In all of the gospel narratives that I have discussed in this chapter on communal scapegoating, none have recreated the notion of two goats, one persecuted and one released/banished—never to be heard from again—until now. Maclean's article thoroughly dives deeply into conceptualizing Jesus and Barabbas embodying the actions/functions of the two goats in Leviticus 16, and she further attempts to make the case that Jesus and Barabbas function to execute the pattern of the Greek curative exit ritual of the scapegoat. This focus on Barabbas may seem strange to most people who see Barabbas as supporting cast in this dramatic court case between Jesus & Pilate, but for scholars, the lack of historical data to support a custom of a Roman governor releasing a prisoner to the Jewish crowd during a festival compels investigation. And then to add to it, the lack of data around Barabbas even heightens the mystery and justifies why

Maclean focuses on this most fascinating interpretive lens to understand the scripture.

But before we get to the juicy part of the narrative, let's begin with the actual exchange between Jesus and Pilate. All four gospels have Jesus in trial against Pilate; and in each gospel, from the very outset, we see the judicially incestuous relationship between the Jewish leaders (i.e., the Sanhedrin) and Pilate. Biblical scholar Raymond Brown notes the close relationship between Pilate and Caiaphas, the high priest along with the rest of the Sanhedrin. At the outset of the trial in Matthew and Mark, once the Sanhedrin turn Jesus over, first Pilate asks Jesus, is He King of the Jews, then the chief priests hurl all manner of accusations against Jesus, but in Luke's version, after rising as a body and handing Him over to Pilate, the Sanhedrin immediately accuse Jesus of acts of sedition, then Pilate questions Jesus, "Are you King of the Jews?" Once Pilate hears Jesus' answer, "You say so," Luke's gospel puts on display this tug of war between Pilate, who believes in Jesus' innocence, and the chief priests and crowds, who are determined to pressure the high court to condemn Jesus. In John's version of the beginning of the trial, Pilate's first words are to the Sanhedrin, who are waiting outside Pilate's headquarters, and he asks them, "What charges are you bringing against Jesus?" If the nature of the symbiotic relationship between the Jewish aristocracy and the Roman government is somewhat veiled in the synoptic versions of the beginning of the trial between Jesus and the Jews, it is in John's version of the narrative that this demented collusion between strange bedfellows is laid bare. The NRSV of John 18:30 translates, "They answered, 'If this man were not a criminal, we would not have handed him over to you.'" In these 16 words, the Jewish leaders expose the rigged criminal justice system for what it is. The Sanhedrin remind Pilate of the nature of the function of the economic and political colonialist systems under Roman rule. This is not about checks and balances. This is not levels of accountability ensuring that there is no abuse. Corruption is the lubricant that oils the machine, so it runs efficiently, and violent scapegoating of black and brown bodies is the high-octane biofuel that allows the machine to perform at high levels. Under Roman rule, Jews were at the mercy of a rich aristocracy who instituted peace through horrific political repression. This is the rich attempting to trigger a Roman ruler to unleash the raw brutality and domination at the heart of its government's DNA as it pertains to Roman occupation in Israel. The violent regime has never hesitated to show its dominance whenever needed. The statement by the Jewish leaders is the very essence of scapegoating. In effect they are saying, Pilate you know the drill, our bringing Jesus to you is not to determine innocence or guilt, that has already been predetermined, since you know that we wouldn't bring this man to you unless he was a threat. So, execute your brutality, unleash your terror, and send the message that anyone considered a threat to our system of exploitation will be demonized, criminalized, and condemned. As Michelle Alexander notes in *The New Jim Crow*: "The parade of guilty people through America's courtrooms gives the false impression to the public—as well as to the judges—that when the police have a "hunch," it makes sense to let them act on it. Judges tend to imagine that the police have a sixth sense—or some kind of special police training—that qualifies them to identify . . . criminals in the absence of any evidence. After all, they seem to be right so much of the time, don't they?"

Yet in all four gospel narratives, Pilate doesn't automatically assume Jesus is guilty just because the Jewish "police" bring Jesus to him. In Luke's gospel, Pilate tries to get out of sentencing a man "under Herod's jurisdiction" (Luke 23:6) by sending him to Herod, who questioned Jesus, yet received no answers. The barrage of accusations (a feature found in all four gospels) hurled at Jesus from the Jewish leaders both in Pilate's trial and in Herod's questioning is reminiscent of the sins heaped on the innocent scapegoat in Leviticus 16. Herod and his soldiers are then recorded as mocking and humiliating Him and dressing Him in an elegant robe in true scapegoat fashion before sending Him back to Pilate. Luke's version conveys the notion that this shuttling back and forth of Jesus transforms their relationship from enemies to friends. Here again, is further evidence of various elements of the criminal justice system working in coordination (even if inadvertently) to scapegoat Jesus. In John's gospel, the religious police are agitated that Pilate dares to question them to name their accusations or charges against Jesus. Such agitation is indicative of a relationship where the Sanhedrin and the Roman procurator have a bad history of collusion when justice was dispensed in criminal court.

In the Sanhedrin trial, the leaders try to pouch Jesus into incriminating Himself, but He refuses. In Pilate's trial, the agent of the governor challenges

Jesus to respond to the charges of His accusers, but again, Jesus refuses to fall for the trap. The limited number of Jesus' words, and the willful decision to not directly answer questions asked of Him in both trials speak to an unwillingness of the Son of God to lend credibility to this phony criminal justice system. Jesus was acutely aware of His status as a criminal condemned before any judicial proceedings commenced, and because He understood His role of fulfilling divine prophecy to suffer as a scapegoat. Unlike Peter striking Caiaphas' servant with the sword, Jesus was not going to resist the course of events already in motion. Unfortunately, the same judicial strategies that were used to convict Jesus are still in play today, and when it is abundantly clear that the fix is in, our best defense is to follow the example of Jesus and not retaliate in kind, but to expose the criminal justice system for what it has historically been for black and brown people: a mechanism to overcharge us with crimes, and shape policy and practices in ways to deny us access to constitutional rights that are normally afforded to other Americans.

Scholars have taken special note of the attitude, behavior, and words of Pilate. What makes pinning down a definitive position complicated is that the gospels are not uniform in their portrayal of Pilate. Was he truly discerning of Jesus' innocence and trying to wiggle out of convicting the Messiah (the synoptics' portrayal of Him), or was he both antagonistic and scornful of the Jews and yet embracing political expediency by initially appearing to dissuade the crowd from their desire to murder Jesus, only to ultimately give the people what they want (John's portrayal of Him)?

Nailing down precisely what was going on in Pilate's head as he queried Jesus may be impossible, but at the end of the day, the Jewish leaders were successful in inciting the crowd to pressure Pilate to release Barabbas, a convicted insurrectionist and murderer who was commuted a death sentence, and sentence Jesus based on false witnesses and testimony, to be crucified. Scholars are divided on whether the gospels succeed in trying to effectively delineate culpability between Pilate, the Jewish leaders, and the crowd. Matthew and Mark go out of their way to show the differentiation between the chief priests of the Sanhedrin and the crowd by spelling out that the former provoked the latter to seal the fate of each of the two "criminals." And yet, their characterization of Pilate in terms of responsibility for the scapegoating of Jesus is not identical. By introducing the washing of his hands, accompanied by an exchange of words while performing that act, Matthew's Pilate attempts to distance himself from the murder of Jesus, even as he delivers Jesus to His accusers who crucify Him, a key detail not found in Mark's version. Along with the wife of Pilate informing him to not harm Jesus, another detail not found in Mark's gospel, they together seem to indicate a deliberate attempt to soften Roman culpability. Luke's version of the trial has the chief priests, leaders, and the crowd reacting in unison as one community persistently pressuring Pilate. They insist on the release of Barabbas and the execution of Jesus (fulfilling one of the key factors of the scapegoat mechanism), whereas John's version never mentions the crowd in the Pilate trial, preferring to refer to the members of the Sanhedrin as the Jews who engage back and forth with Pilate. John's Pilate has no shame initially in violently persecuting Jesus and ridiculing the Jews, referring to Jesus as the King of the Jews to them, having Him flogged, putting a crown on His head and dressing Him in a purple robe. We know that scapegoats in the practice of the scapegoat ritual of Leviticus 16, and in other nonbiblical traditions were treated similarly. After Pilate learns that the justification for killing Jesus by the Jews is the accusation that He claims to be the Son of God, John's gospel acknowledges that Pilate's fear grew. When Jesus refuses to respond to the question, "Where do you come from," it prompts Pilate to remind Jesus of his power. Scapegoating at its essence is about power, but the power is volatile and sometimes the ones who scapegoat underestimate the power of the scapegoat itself. In response to Pilate's declaration of his power, Jesus educates Pilate as to who really is in charge (John 19:11), and from that point forward Pilate begins to sense the power of Jesus and attempts to release Jesus, but the Jews would not have any of it.

Two Scapegoats or a Scapegoat and Immolated Goat Personified

Ultimately, we must take time to look at the apparent symmetry between the two goats in Leviticus 16 and Barabbas and Jesus, the two criminals in the gospels who are put up by Pilate for the crowd to choose. The formation of the dispensing of justice for Jesus and Barabbas perfectly objectifies two individuals as though they were nonhuman, one being treated as an offering of appeasement (to de-escalate the frenzy of the crowd/Jewish leaders) and the other upon whom guilt was unjustly piled. Collectively the intertwined judicial rulings appear to neatly fit the scapegoat ritual of Leviticus 16. Many scholars note that Matthew's gospel goes out of its way to depict Jesus and Barabbas as more similar than different; he characterizes both of their sir names as Jesus, and Matthew's Pilate introduces the crowd to Barabbas as an alternative to execute, whereas the other gospels more directly have the crowd initiate the demand for the release of Barabbas. Furthermore, both could be considered criminals charged with insurrection; one insurrectionist was notably associated with murder, while the other was a rebel aiming to dismantle Jewish oligarchy and whose movement, started after his death, was seen as a threat to Roman hegemony. Maclean also creates symmetry between Jesus and Barabbas when she posits that "either prisoner . . . would threaten priestly power and it is difficult to see why priests would prefer one over the other." Multiple scholars have deduced that Barabbas was a threat to the chief priests because an insurrection against Rome would signal to Rome the inability of the priests to maintain order and contain threats. Thus, they would be forced to brutalize Jews indiscriminately, which ultimately happened when Rome decimated Jerusalem in 70 AD. However additional context is important here, to create essential contrast between these two potential scapegoats. In attempting to get us to consider Barabbas as the scapegoat and Jesus as the immolated goat, Jennifer K. Berenson Maclean in her important scholarly article neglects to see Jesus abused as "a scapegoat to the point of death while being led out of the city in a ritualized procession by members of the community." Do the gospels show Jesus being abused from the trial until his death? Yes. Was he led out of the city in a ritualized fashion? If we can call the process of Roman crucifixion ritualistic as the gospels chronicle Jesus being led to Golgotha and the spectacle that the process drew to get members of the community to watch, yes!

The elements of the scapegoat ritual and the Greco-Roman curative rites, which Maclean wants to use as a lens to view the scapegoating of Jesus and Barabbas in the gospel narratives, are present in the life of Jesus the Christ throughout His biological existence, not just at the very end. This whole chapter is a testament to confirming Jesus' qualifications to embody what it means to be a scapegoat from the cradle to the cross, whereas for Barabbas, we have little to no data outside the trial with Pilate. As Maclean notes, after he is released, Barabbas mysteriously fades into invisibility, never to be mentioned again in scripture, so despite her eager attempts to use exegesis as a means to garner support for seeing Barabbas as a scapegoat who was released for the mob to violate, there is no detailed description of what happens to Barabbas to corroborate such an unpopular analysis. On the other hand, we have rich data for the true scapegoat Jesus, who was criminalized and demonized throughout His ministry. Despite Maclean's insistence that Barabbas could be considered the "true Christian scapegoat before Jesus was (I'm struggling to discern what is 'Christian' about the notion of releasing Barabbas to the crowd for them to scapegoat him)," it is Jesus who embodies the elements of the curative exit rites. He was a threat (the gospels make that point repeatedly in multiple ways), and His status transforms (from Son of Man to Son of God) over the course of the rite. He engages in ritual action that concentrates and directs divine power, He is banished from multiple communities, and when crucified we say in the Apostles Creed, that He descended to hell toward the enemy, and His violent death on one level functioned to divert disaster (Romans violently oppressing Jews), of which it failed, but on a spiritual level His action diverted the disaster of eternal damnation for all sinners who accept Jesus as their personal Savior. I think Cyril of Alexandria hit the nail on the head; as Son of Man, Jesus is the scapegoat of Leviticus 16, a man who was seen as a threat from birth, suffered throughout His ministry and demonized while ordained to carry the sins of all of us. On the other hand, as Son of God, Jesus is the immolated goat of Leviticus 16, whose violent death purifies our spiritual connection and appeases God's desire to be intimate with humanity.

Examining Scapegoating in the Suffering of Christ at Calvary

At last, we focus on the crucifixion of Jesus. In the Black tradition, when people say Christianity is a white man's religion, they gloss over the reality of how deeply the suffering of Jesus on the cross resonates with the suffering of black people. As a collective, we may not customarily refer to our suffering (or Jesus' suffering) from the lens of the scapegoat mechanism, but regardless, on a visceral level, we authentically empathize with being a victim of unjustified communal violence. "The expression scapegoat is not used (in the gospels), but the gospels have a perfect substitute in the Lamb of God. Like scapegoat, it implies the substitute of one victim for all the others but replaces all the distasteful and loathsome connotations of the goat with the positive associations of the lamb. It indicates more clearly the innocence of the victim, the injustice of the condemnation, and the causelessness of the hatred of which it is the object."

The cross of Christ represents the pinnacle of scapegoating in that the suffering endured was undeserved and yet carried for the sake of the sins of many. The grotesque mistreatment however is met with resolute defiance as Jesus, who in Luke and John particularly is depicted as in control from the first statement, "Father forgive them for they know not what they are doing," through the last word, "It is finished." The notion of them (the scapegoaters who put Him on the cross) not knowing the ramifications of their actions, speaks to there being much more occurring than what we glean from the physical realm; a point, I will elaborate on in further detail later in this work. How Jesus responds to the scapegoating is insightful because it demonstrates that in the midst of suffering, opportunities for empowerment exist (Jesus promises to one of the criminals crucified that they would join Him in paradise, and He redefines family by uniting His mother Mary with the beloved disciple John). It is insightful because it demonstrates Jesus' awareness that the brutality of the Roman soldiers (police) plays right into God's agenda of defeating evil using its own strategy, and it is insightful because the scapegoater (centurion) saw how Jesus endured the dehumanization and declared Him innocent (Luke 23:47). Recognizing the centurion praising God and declaring Jesus Christ's innocence hearkens back to the victory of the Suffering Servant in Isaiah 53, and when Joseph says to his brothers in Genesis 50:20, "you meant evil against me, but God meant it for good."

CHAPTER 5

GEORGE FLOYD THE SCAPEGOAT/ LAMB IN GENESIS/LEVITICUS, ISAIAH, AND THE GOSPELS

Having teased out the nature of communal scapegoating in Leviticus (through Genesis), Isaiah, and in the gospels, what we have uncovered is that all through the Bible, people have consistently used the tool of scapegoating, having no issues transferring blame onto either an animal or someone deemed deserving, which for them, justifies wielding violent suffering when motivated, to accomplish their purposes. The question is how does George Floyd relate to these scapegoating narratives in the Bible? Are there relevant points of intersection between the murder of George Floyd (and by extension, many other unarmed victims of police brutality) including its aftermath and the insights these scriptures have yielded?

For me, the answer is an emphatic yes and again, it is the sole reason behind this publication; to get folks to discover and affirm how the Bible speaks through the scapegoat mechanism to the chronic issue of police using excessive force when engaging with certain demographics in society. What happens to us is not new, it's grounded in the Word of God, and the more we see our sufferings through the suffering of the scapegoats of scripture, the more we can draw strength not just to endure but to thrive in spite of the ongoing perversion of justice we continually face.

Connecting the Scapegoating in Leviticus 16 with George Floyd's Murder/Aftermath

Looking at the disputed origins for the divine policy instituted in Leviticus 16, seeing that its formation is likely tied to Genesis' narrative of conflict between Joseph and his brothers, helps us frame a perspective of recognizing how unjustified violence can suddenly become justified and sanctioned by a community. In other words, possibly the best way to make the connection of George Floyd's murder with the scapegoat ritual in Leviticus 16 is to first show its connection to the scapegoat scandal in Genesis between Joseph and his brothers. George Floyd was accused of attempting to pass counterfeit currency in a store, by all accounts, a crime; Joseph was accused of unjustly provoking his brothers by sharing with them dreams of them serving him, which along with their father's favoritism, caused them to detest him. The manufacturing of criminality is a hallmark feature that functions to trigger and facilitate the justification of violence upon the scapegoat. At first glance, one would say that criminals need to be punished and therefore the violence serves as just punishment for the criminal. But in reality, the criminality in the Genesis narrative regarding Joseph is a figment of imagination. The brothers embellish Joseph's infraction such that it becomes larger than life and compels the brothers to employ violence to arrest the favoritism of Joseph by their father—a corruption that apparently is infecting the sacredness of the sons' relationship with their father. In Leviticus, the damage of wanton, unrepentant sin of the community, has defiled the inner sanctum and severed the Israelites' relationship with God, so much so that violence inflicted upon the immolated goat offered to God and also to the sent away goat offered to Azazel, function in ways similar to the violence Joseph's brothers inflict upon him to repair and cleanse the family dynamic between father and sons. With George Floyd, the behavior of Derek Chauvin was a nod commemorating the actions of Joseph's brothers by embellishing the alleged wrongdoing of George Floyd; his actions portraying righteous indignation baked in fear. Fear is a textbook catalyst for activating the identification and targeting of a scapegoat that a group can victimize via sanctioned violence. What did the brothers fear? That the dreamer's dream would come true; that one day, Joseph was to reign and have dominion over his brothers (Genesis 37:8). Derek Chauvin is the one police officer who executed George Floyd, but he had three other officers who assisted him and were complicit in the murder of George Floyd. Most telling, Derek Chauvin is a representative of a corrupt law enforcement system that since the very first Slave Patrols in the Carolina counties in 1702, has consistently operated out of fear. Fear of what? That freed blacks may one day rule and seek revenge for the suffering endured, sometimes covertly, but often overtly underneath the guise of maintaining white supremacy. Dr. Potter underscores this notion of fear in the development of police departments in the South whose original function was Slave Patrol, but "following the Civil War, these vigilante-style organizations evolved into modern Southern police departments primarily as a means of controlling freed slaves who were now laborers working in an agricultural caste system, and enforcing "Jim Crow" segregation laws, designed to deny freed slaves equal rights and access to the political system."

There is another connecting factor between George Floyd and Joseph that is primordial in nature. Joseph was the 11th of 12 sons born to Jacob and Rachel, and in part, because Jacob had Joseph while he was relatively old, he favored Joseph over his other sons. His favoring Joseph influenced Jacob giving Joseph a coat of many colors (Genesis 37:3). These two elements, being favored and being given a coat of ornate colors, I consider primordial or existing from the very outset, in that they fuel the triggering of the scapegoat scandal later in the narrative. George Floyd's primordial factor that triggers him becoming a scapegoat is being a black man in America. The sad truth is that while the use of excessive force by police against unarmed black men has been an enduring legacy in this country, it took the concrete lynching of a black man on the ground, handcuffed with a knee on his neck for over nine minutes before many in the world saw the obvious, that no such mistreatment would ever be considered justifiable for a white person in a similar circumstance. These primordial factors, of which the protagonists in each of the narratives have no control over, are the driving force that triggers the communities (Joseph's brothers and the Minneapolis police) to scapegoat Joseph and George Floyd respectively.

Joseph's brothers are so seething in hostility at Joseph, because of their father's favoritism towards him, that they at first contemplate killing Joseph, but eventually settle for throwing him into a ditch in the wilderness (a compelling connection with the scapegoat being sent away into the wilderness in Leviticus 16:21-22) and ultimately selling him (as a slave) to the Midianites. Comparatively, Derek Chauvin becomes so internally enraged with George Floyd, possibly for multiple reasons, but undoubtedly because something about being black triggers an all-encompassing fear and hatred in some white men, that he pins down the suspect with the assistance of his fellow officers and proceeds to put his knee on George Floyd's neck until he is dead. The sense that the brothers' motives of violent assault were for a good cause (to prevent Jacob from showing favoritism and instead loving his sons equitably) resonates with law enforcement's use of unjustifiable excessive force for the "righteous" cause of rooting out the criminal element of the community in Minneapolis. It has been noted that "transporting a load of Israelite toxic waste, consisting of moral faults, to Azazel in the wilderness and abandoning it there by the command of Yahweh" in Leviticus 16 is uniquely designed to neutralize the scapegoat scandal of Joseph's brothers. This transfer of culpability is a hallmark feature of scapegoating showcased in Genesis, as the brothers shift evil on multiple levels. They shift the evil of their actions upon Joseph by blaming him for their violent assault upon him and they shift the evil of their action upon the goat by killing it in the name of using it as a cover for their violence upon Joseph. Joseph and the goat in Genesis are both manipulated to transfer and send evil and culpability away from Joseph's brothers. The divine lawgiver in Leviticus 16 picks up on this duality of double scapegoats from the Genesis narrative, with one scapegoat being sent away while the other is immolated. In the case of George Floyd, there is no presence of two distinct scapegoats as in Genesis and in Leviticus 16, but the concrete lynching of "the scapegoat" attempts to criminalize/demonize one who is deemed guilty and using what was historically characterized summary justice to cleanse or purge the community from its unrighteousness.

Summary Justice is when someone or a community feels emboldened to act as judge, jury, and executioner long before due process and the presumption of innocence until proven guilty is ever considered. Of course, the police department's version of cleansing and purging via summary justice is warped as it is incubated in the legacy of suppressing black and brown people from obtaining independence from the control of ruling elites, one of the historic tenets of the formation of police departments in the South, according to Dr. Gary Potter in his scholarly article entitled the *History of Policing in the United States.* Whereas the scapegoat offered to Azazel in Leviticus 16 is sent away to create the isolation of corruptive elements away from the community to sanitize it, the agenda of isolating bad individuals (a la George Floyd) in the name of crime control away from society to protect it from corruption of criminality has justified the use of excessive force since the formation of police departments, especially in the South. In many ways, police brutality has used the nefarious motives of Joseph's brothers, (or Rene Girard would say the same mimetic desires) cloaked in the language of cleansing, purging and restoring community, to curry the collective sanctioning of violence on targeted individuals of a certain skin color. And for the most part, the fear of allowing crime to go unpunished and the convincing by law enforcement that police officers needed qualified immunity in order to effectively keep the peace have joined together to give law enforcement the right to violently scapegoat black and brown bodies for decades if not centuries with hardly any recourse.

The conflation of both human and animal scapegoating in Genesis by Joseph's brothers against him is a significant revelation that has profound implications for how biblical scapegoating relates to the death of George Floyd and countless other unarmed black and brown bodies by law enforcement. By handcuffing him behind his back, pinning him down face-first to the concrete, and pressing the knee against the neck for over nine minutes, police officers collectively treated George Floyd like some human beings treat animals.

Connecting the Scapegoating in Isaiah 53 with George Floyd in 2020

The mistreatment of the Suffering Servant in Isaiah, became the catalyst for the servants' recognition that the Servant did nothing to deserve His affliction. Prior to the persecution and death of the Servant, the servants speak of the Servant as one who was appropriately disregarded, but as the victimization intensified and ultimately led to death, the cataracts that blinded the truth fell, and an unprecedented clarity of vision was attained. God's magic took evil's agenda and used it to execute the beauty of holiness. "The work of the servant required God's illumination to lift it out of the realm of brute facts and into the realm of saving providence. Otherwise, it was just another death among deaths, another case of picking on the weak and undesirable, another instance of some good man going wrongly to the grave, done in by a corrupt justice system." For me, this indicates that the scapegoat or Suffering Servant has been elevated to become a lamb. "In the report about the servant's death, the witnesses state certain truths that they are absolutely convicted of, (which) arise out of a passionate rehearsal of a truth that has grasped them, not one that they are grasping. God has acted in such a way as to convict those who had convicted the despised of the fragility of any assumptions, they once upon a time, held so boldly and unswervingly; and God has raided their sensibility and intellect in the work of the servant, transforming and baptizing them toward the deepest perception of divine truth and intention. So now, within the report they give, the witnesses speak of the truth that has come upon them and loosed their tongues for a different sort of report than they had ever before given." This new revelation of truth, which catapults the Suffering Servant to triumph and even causes the perpetrators of the suffering to triumph, not only because they see the truth of their own agency in the suffering of the Servant, but also because they recognize the saving power truth brings to them as it brings triumph to the oppressed. This notion of suffering which redeems the oppressed and saves the oppressor is at the essence of what I call the theology of the lamb. It is this unmistakable, undeniable reality that the more vicious the violation of the vulnerable is waged, the greater the clarity of the mistreatment and the surer the strength of truth prevails. The more haters try to scapegoat, the more absurd the false narratives which epically fail to justify the violence become.

The awakening to the truth in terms of the nature of the suffering for the Servant is so closely theologically and metaphysically related to the suffering of George Floyd. White folk all across the world who couldn't or wouldn't see the truth with Tamir Rice, Michael Brown, Trayvon Martin, and so many others, finally began to see it. Hallelujah, they saw the truth. Systemic racism is alive and well. One of the titles for my sermon, no doubt a result of wrestling with this notion of scapegoating in Isaiah 53 was "We Have Met the Enemy and the Enemy Is Us." Some had seen the ugliness of police brutality waged disproportionately on black and brown bodies before and joined the cause to defeat it. Others saw it before George Floyd, but refused to see their own agency, their own privilege. Still, others fell into the trap of "what did the black man do to provoke the officers" mentality. The murder of George Floyd for legions of white folk made all those excuses nonsensical. The multitude of videos from a plethora of perspectives, exposing the inhumane treatment by the officers were condemning. The symphony of law enforcement leaders who loudly cried foul before the trial and those who testified during the trial, from the crisis intervention trainer all the way up to the Police Chief of Minneapolis, they all characterized the violence inflicted by the officers as completely unnecessary and uncalled for. But it's not a few bad apples in a police department, it is systemic. This shift in revelation is what makes the killing of George Floyd sacrificial and triumphant. All scapegoating is sacrificial but not all sacrifice is triumphant. George Floyd's sacrifice, like the Suffering Servant that became a lamb in Isaiah 53, is triumphant. His murder has substantially changed the narrative globally in ways that other killings of black and brown bodies simply didn't. My statement is not meant to diminish the lives of the tens of thousands, probably hundreds of thousands of victims of violent, communal, state-sponsored scapegoating. But George Floyd's murder unlike so many others, was able to withstand intense critique still shift the paradigm. This is why I characterize his death as transforming him from scapegoat to lamb. Not because of anything he did, but because God chose to do so. Is he a martyr? My definition of a martyr is one who foresees the suffering and embraces it. George Floyd didn't choose suffering; he was forced to suffer and in so doing he triumphed like a lamb.

When Christian theology recognizes Isaiah 53 as one of its pillars for seeing Jesus as the Messiah that fulfills Old Testament prophecy, it should be no wonder then that black people gravitate to honor and hallow the one who chose to suffer as we have been forced to suffer. Many have tried to denounce and debunk Christianity in an effort to get descendants of Africans to embrace "a more African religion," but the reality is, it is the oneness of suffering, the legacy of humans of a dark hue being bastardized as void of beauty and attraction (Isaiah 53:2), the history of being despised and rejected, dishonored and discarded (Isaiah 53:3), the notion of having iniquity and punishment heaped on us unjustly (Isaiah 53:5,7), the sense of being a defenseless lamb led to the slaughter (Isaiah 53:7), the reality of being taken away and cut off from the land (Isaiah 53:8)—all of these sensibilities of being scapegoated in this Messianic chapter boldly prophesy of the violence that black and brown bodies including George Floyd have endured that force us to mirror the reality of the victimization of the Suffering Servant.

And then add to it, the notion that on a rare occasion, a senseless killing like George Floyd's murder causes privileged voices to be silenced and for their eyes to see events in ways never seen before (Isaiah 52:15) is God creating *Kairos* in the midst of chaos. But when they do speak, they utter a realization that their previous understandings of the suffering servant(s) were wrong! These same dynamics of suffering compelling new vision were at play as a result of the murder of George Floyd as well. Our understanding that God had afflicted "him" or "her" and created them as inherently corrupt was flawed. That the suffering servant(s)' pain was caused by the privileged and their wrongdoing, but equally important that it took seeing the suffering for the transformation of understanding to take place. The healing that takes place is not just on a spiritual level but on a social and mental one as well as the death of the suffering servant(s) causes a cataclysmic recalibration of mentalities and behaviors that could not happen separate and apart from the violent, sacred, undeserved sacrifice. Behold the Lamb of God that was slain, who triumphed in death.

King Herod Scapegoats the Male Babies in Bethlehem

To project forward from King Herod's scapegoating of innocent babies of Bethlehem in Matthew's gospel, who are hunted and targeted based on their location, I am saddened to recognize how some police officers operate from the same mentality toward black and brown bodies based on their location. Bethlehem during the time of Jesus was a small town of little to no prominence when Jesus was born, but upon hearing of the birth of the one born King of the Jews, the king was troubled and all of Jerusalem with him. The text infers a collective identification of a threat and the king issues an order to ensure that the threat is violently neutralized.

The killing of George Floyd in Minneapolis is indicative of the way police officers in nonaffluent neighborhoods routinely characterize black people as threats, which hearkens back to the history of police functioning as slave patrols and aligns with King Herod scapegoating the babies of Bethlehem.

I have seen numerous debates about whether Jesus became a refugee when Joseph slips the holy family into Egypt due to Herod's edict to slaughter the children, an event some refer to as the Massacre of the Innocents. Some say that at the time, Herod had jurisdiction over Egypt in addition to Bethlehem but regardless, even if Egypt was under Roman Empire at the time of Jesus' birth, Herod had enough sense not to slaughter male babies in Egypt!

Ironically, black men and women in affluent neighborhoods are not immune to being seen as a threat, but by and large, they are not targeted for violence by the authorities with laser-like precision like black and brown folks from less affluent neighborhoods are. I find this particularly ironic, because the usual justification for why extra attention is being paid by police to less affluent neighborhoods is crime. But the reality is, a case could be made that the power affluent blacks hold could be perceived as more of a threat than the danger associated with the crimes prevalent in less affluent neighborhoods. Yet the use of excessive force by the police is disproportionately seen in less affluent neighborhoods. King Herod's fixation on neutralizing a perceived threat that leads to exterminating male babies from a specific location has tentacles that resonate with how some police officers use crime as a scapegoat to prey upon black and brown bodies in less affluent neighborhoods today.

When Activities on the Sabbath Turn into a Justification to Scapegoat Jesus

In countless deaths of unarmed black individuals, those who have privilege to act like the authority have often characterized the behavior of the victims as threatening. A kid of a certain skin complexion with a hoodie walking home becomes the definition of a threat. A jog in an upscale neighborhood becomes the definition of a threat or criminality. Running away is a threat and lying on the ground, face-first, hands cuffed behind the back will be considered in the case of the police officers involved in the murder of George Floyd a threat. This work is not an attempt to blindly reject every instance in which violence against black and brown bodies takes place. Clearly, there are times when violence may be justified. Worst case, even if we could definitively assert that Jesus violated the Sabbath, how does that justify the plot to kill him? An arrest? Okay. A court appearance? Okay; but to plot to kill is without debate, over the top. Yet this same demented thought process often plays itself out in the use of excessive force by police officers confronting black and brown individuals. Even if George Floyd passed counterfeit money, which was never proven, what did he do to deserve a knee on top of his neck for over nine minutes? The same overreaction in the gospels of the Pharisees toward Jesus, is the same overreaction of police officers to many unarmed black individuals confronted about alleged criminal activity. How is it that alleged criminals of white complexion who have been suspected of killing people in cold blood (Dylan Roof) are driven to go get something to eat before being detained and processed, but black and brown bodies who are suspected of less are characterized as a threat that leads too often to violent scapegoating?

As much as we can easily judge the Pharisees for being obsessed with Sabbath violation and neglecting the value of Jesus making a man whole, how many Christian sanctuaries are willing to humanize the hurting and allow the nonglamorous work of healing to take place in the middle of our Sabbath worship services? Are we agents of Jesus, who came to recover sight to the blind, liberate those who are bound, preach good news to the broken-hearted by ministering to their physical and mental wounds even on our celebrated Sabbath, or do we operate more aligned with Pharisees, and basically tell the hurting who need healing that it is inappropriate to address their issues on "our Sabbath" and instead bid the poor and needy to come back during the weekday office hours? We can point the finger at the Pharisees and crucify them for their exploitation of criminalization to scapegoat, yet we neglect to see how too many churches today use our celebrated Sabbath to scapegoat those Rev. Dr. Charles G. Adams calls the least, the last, the lost, the little, the unlucky and the left out.

Demonization Used as a Tool to Scapegoat

When seen as a threat, demonization is one of the preferred tools used to proactively justify scapegoating or reactively interpret a context as fearful to justify deploying violence. In the gospels, I mentioned in chapter four that Jesus is demonized by His own family (Mark 3:21) as well as the Pharisees (Mark 3:20-30, Matthew 12:22-32, and Luke 11:14-23) by maligning His disposition. Detractors of George Floyd immediately rushed to malign his character and in the trial of Derek Chauvin, we learned that the officers and at least one other witness on the scene who testified believed that George Floyd was on drugs (which could otherwise be characterized as being demon-possessed). In watching the trial of Derek Chauvin, the presumption that George Floyd was under the influence of drugs which maligned his character, justified the excessive use of force, and that the drugs were the overwhelming factor that caused his death was critical to the defense's case of creating a context of the police feeling threatened by him.

The reality is in scripture, more often than not, those who scapegoat others are themselves full of demons that need to be exorcised. Joseph's brothers demonize Joseph and use it as justification to scapegoat him, when in reality, it is the brothers who themselves are demon-possessed with unclean spirits, and as blind and as full of rage as Cain was toward his brother Abel, in the first violent scapegoating in scripture. Post-Leviticus 16, it is the Israelites themselves, who heap their sins, their iniquities, their demons onto the scapegoat in the first place. The goat is innocent, but the transfer of sins to the scapegoat over time became a license to blame the goat. In Isaiah 53, the servants report that their amazement of the realization that the Suffering Servant is innocent and a victim of marginalization on behalf of and because of them, is a confession of their own scapegoating of the Suffering Servant, as well as their own demons that cause the affliction of the Servant. The Pharisees follow the same pattern as the other biblical characters who scapegoat. They are quick to call Jesus demon-possessed so they can violate Him, while unable to perceive their own hypocrisy (Matthew 23:13, 15), their own blindness (John 9:40), in essence, their own demon-possession. Suffice it to say that the police officers who encountered George Floyd, perceived that he was under the influence of "demons," yet were clueless about their own demon-possession, which the world was able to see in full display that dreadful day. And yet, I dare say that the Minneapolis police department, like other departments across the country, has had to engage with nonblack members of the community who battle drug addiction and somehow those members are able to live to see another day. The only explanation that makes sense to me is that the high white supremacy provides is far more potent and addictive than any chemical substance found in George Floyd's body that day.

The Gerasene demoniac passages in scripture also draw parallels to the scapegoating of George Floyd. In the sermon series, "When Life Drives Us Crazy," I spoke to the dichotomy or irony of the Gerasene demoniac technically being alive but overwhelmed in a context of tombs and death. Demonization in this regard becomes a de facto license to create a dysfunctional equilibrium where people relegate a certain demographic to a cycle of powerlessness, where they are redlined, chained, shackled, and quarantined to abide in a context consumed by death and tombs. They make attempts to free themselves from bondage, and signs indicating an external hint of progress toward that goal may surface, but the psychic and emotional imprisonment manifested internally renders them incapable of freeing themselves. The failure to fully emancipate from bondage even if the chains are not literal, eventually causes the victims to "howl and cut themselves with stones," which prompts the community to come out and chain the demon-possessed in the tombs and the cycle repeats over and over.

When I think about it (the juxtaposition of breaking shackles but still battling demons while dwelling in the tombs), I think about the various stages of George Floyd's life, growing up a black man with little options to evade an upbringing filled with violence and death in Houston's 3rd Ward. Despite the incredible odds, George Floyd made multiple attempts to free himself from the cycle, but battling his own demons, he found himself never fully liberated from the tombs, so the cycle continued. His moving of his life from Houston to Minnesota to start over was a strong indication of someone trying to break the cycle, but his demons, and the same overzealous criminal justice system addicted to upholding white supremacy in Houston, met him in Minneapolis. The more he tried to escape the tombs, the more his demons and the police, working on behalf of the community, followed him, tormented him, and eventually, the chronic trauma of living in the tombs took its toll on May 25, 2020. If there is any demographic who knows about going mentally crazy, black people know about the juxtaposition of being previously chained and bound, under the appearance of visual vestiges of being free, but still mentally enslaved. Much like today, "leaving prison after a felony conviction but much of society still deems you unfit to vote, to get a job, to get a business loan, etc. It's enough to drive any man or woman out of their mind." An overzealous criminal justice system, which extends well beyond scapegoating tactics used by police officers, to include, the Justice Department of the Federal Government, the sentencing guidelines utilized by federal, state, and local courts, and the way the criminal justice system for black and brown people functions in comprehensive, coordinated ways to catch and release criminals under the guise of law and order resonates with the chained yet relegated to the tombs dynamic in the Gerasene demoniac narrative that George Floyd understood. As Michelle Alexander, author of *The New Jim Crow*, has so soundly articulated: "Hundreds of thousands of people of color are swept into this (caste) system and released every year, yet we rationalize the systemic discrimination and exclusion and turn a blind eye to the suffering."

In watching the videos from the various body cams of the police officers during the trial of Derek Chauvin, it was clear that the unnecessary escalation of Officer Thomas Lane pulling out his gun and pointing it at George Floyd less than a minute after their initial encounter while Floyd sat in the driver's seat of "his vehicle" traumatized him. He literally pleaded with the officers to de-escalate because he had been triggered by memories of being shot previously. Social workers and medical professionals alike understand this condition as Post Traumatic Stress Disorder. The legion of demons both chemical and visceral rendered him alive and yet haunted when triggered, unable to escape the tombs. In watching the videos from the scene of George Floyd's murder, the way in which the demon-possessed man from Gerasene is trapped in the midst of death is played out for us to see in real time. When Officers Lane and Keung struggle to handcuff Floyd behind his back and have him sit on the ground, Floyd's demeanor temporarily shifts, as if he senses that he may have a chance to escape death if not arrest. Alas, his pseudo-Kairos window of opportunity disappears as quickly as it had appeared as the rookie officers force Floyd to get up and walk with them across the street in order to get him in the squad car. The multiple attempts of the officers to restrain him, the penchant for Floyd to try to evade confinement, the verbal pleading and the actions of Floyd, while being forced into the squad car and then while being dragged out of the car all pay homage to the Gerasene demoniac breaking free from the chains and shackles, then howling and cutting of himself with stones, and being re-shackled. Was it drugs, or his mental condition associated with PTSD, or his mental condition of feeling dehumanized by law enforcement that caused him to resist being confined? The officers and the defense lawyers in the trial exploited the drug use as reason to violently scapegoat "the demon." By choosing that drugs were the root cause of the persistent noncompliance to instructions, the root cause for the paranoia and resistance Floyd displayed, the officers had multiple strategies at their disposal to de-escalate and control the scene, but they chose without justification to escalate the confrontation.

How do we know that the Gerasenes did not genuinely want to restrain the demon-possessed man for his own good but to use shackles as a way to contain and restrict the demon-possessed man from accessing empowerment? How can we be certain that their motive was to scapegoat and exploit rather than empower and uplift? Their hostile response to Jesus' appearance and exorcism, thereby liberating the demon-possessed man from the dysfunctional cycle Mark's gospel describes so vividly, leaves no doubt of their insidious agenda. "One would think that the Gerasenes, if they were in their right mind, they would rejoice when Jesus exorcises the legion! They no longer will need to worry about the former demon-possessed man being tormented. But that is not their response. When they saw the former demoniac sitting there, "clothed and in his right mind," the very man who was previously possessed by the legion, they were afraid. Then they begged Jesus to leave their neighborhood. They realized the cycle they helped design and orchestrate had been broken. The fear in the text is strange, but it only makes sense, if the Gerasenes were comfortable with the dysfunctional cycle. It only makes sense if Jesus has now messed up their program to keep the demon-possessed man surrounded by death in the tombs." "When the (Gerasene demoniac) man is healed, he progresses from the non-human life of a rabid animal to that of a person with a home and friends." The community was angry at Jesus because He overthrew the scapegoat mechanism that had kept an outcast dehumanized. The text goes out of its way to express complete solidarity of the community in its feelings towards Jesus. The system was functioning precisely as it was designed to function, until Jesus overturned it.

Similarly, the "community of blue" functioned in perfect solidarity that day refusing to entertain anyone, offering to shut down their collective scapegoating, even an off-duty firefighter, who initially offered to render medical care but was negated. After being denied the public servant persisted in urging the "blue tribe" to at least check his pulse, conveying her commitment to her vow as a frontline first responder to swiftly render medical care when needed. Of the four, you would think that something would have triggered the black cop who had joined the force specifically to reform white cops from brutalizing black people on his third shift on the force, would at some point render aid, yet he renders concern for his buddy Officer Lane, by inquiring about *his* injury. Apparently, Lane had scraped his knee during the altercation with Floyd; meanwhile the knees of Alex Hueng that were smashed into George Floyd's back, certainly impacted Floyd's ability to breathe, and inflicted agony and suffering as Floyd struggled to breathe while pinned to the concrete. "You're fine, you're talking fine." Each time I hear the recording of Floyd wailing in agony as he is murdered for the world to see, for some reason "fine" is not how I would quite describe it. As I intimated before, it reminds me of a version of the howling of the Gerasene demoniac in the tombs . . . definitely not "fine."

Darrow Jones, childhood friend of Alex Keung, spoke of their disagreement about police this way: "Our fundamental disagreement around law enforcement is not that I believe cops are bad people. I just believe that the system needs to be completely wiped out and replaced. It's the difference between reform and rebuilding." "How do you as an individual think that you're going to be able to change that system, especially when you're going in at a low level?" said Michelle Gross, president of Communities United Against Police Brutality in Minneapolis. "You're not going to feel OK to say, 'Stop, senior officer.' The culture is such, that that kind of intervening would be greatly discouraged."

A Criminal Justice System Masters the Art of Scapegoating

When protesters and onlookers of demonstrations to end police brutality ask, why are they (the police) dressed as if they are fighting rebels in a third world country, I wonder do they recognize how their utterances tap into the prophetic words of Jesus spoken thousands of years ago when He said to the armed mob who arrested Him, "Have you come out with swords and clubs to arrest me as though I were a bandit?" (Matthew 26:55/Mark 14:48). Jesus' question foreshadows both the sentiment of the confrontation George Floyd had with a gun drawn on him seconds after encountering police, and the feelings of the protestors of marches against police using excessive force who have been confronted by militarized law enforcement officers. Hear the righteous indignation in the language of blogger Isaiah just days after George Floyd's death, "As some dared to express their outrage (of the murder of George Floyd) through protest, (Minneapolis Police Department) MPD decided to meet this public grief with escalation and more violence (which as we have seen in multiple police jurisdictions across the country, is not specific to Minneapolis). The MPD turns our peaceful protests into warzones by shooting teargas, flash grenades, and rubber bullets into crowds of Minneapolis residents indiscriminately. The only response they have to our shared grief and anger of the violence they commit against us is more violence. They have chosen a path of escalation and brutality over community and safety."

How is the escalation of violence justified? The men and women in blue within police departments across the country are submerged into a culture that seduces them into seeing protestors and black and brown "suspects" just as the angry mob saw Jesus; threats that justify and authorize them to use violent scapegoating. Whether it is confronting a person of color individually or dealing with passionate protestors as a group, militarizing the police escalates the engagement prematurely, undercuts the mission of protecting and serving, and unnecessarily provides easier access to the "privilege" of violently scapegoating without accountability. In multiple places in this publication, I have raised this dichotomy within the art of scapegoating, whereby the scapegoaters transfer their own guilt to their victims, and then castigate the victim for the very iniquities the scapegoaters gave them. The police officers believed that George Floyd was high, but is it not our criminal justice system that has become high off of scapegoating black and brown bodies, to feed its greed for economic revenues generated from mass incarceration, and to serve the agenda of white supremacy? The defense team in the trial of Derek Chauvin attempted to paint George Floyd as a threat because he is so much bigger than Thomas Lane and Alex Kueng, but the video shows a man who was initially spooked by the surprise encounter, then triggered by the violent escalation when Thomas Lane pointed his gun at George Floyd within seconds of first engaging him. Jesus' words when Judas and the angry mob ambushed and arrested Him are incredibly insightful here: "But Jesus said to them, "Have you come out with swords and clubs, as though I were a criminal, to capture Me?" The defense then attempts to paint the bystanders as an angry coalition hell-bent on potentially harming the officers when in reality they were pleading for the officers to apply the principle of the oath to protect and serve George Floyd. Multiple law enforcement professionals, including the Minneapolis police chief, testified that neither George Floyd nor the crowds were a threat. So, who really was under the influence? Then the defense tried to say that the agitated mob distracted the officers from providing the duty of care all police officers are sworn to uphold. Next, the defense sought to say that there were moments within the dreaded 9 minutes and 29 seconds when Derek Chauvin didn't have his knee on George Floyd's neck, but on other parts of his body, aiming to sell the notion that Derek Chauvin's knee was not the cause of George Floyd's death. But Dr. Martin Tobin, a medical expert specializing in how the human body breathes, suffocated that strategy by flatly stating that a healthy person subjected to what Mr. Floyd was subjected to would have died as a result of what he was subjected to. These are telltale signs of a criminal justice system completely strung out, and like any addict, hallucinating on an alternate reality as well as totally sold out in attempting to get us to believe the alternate universe despite the preponderance of evidence indicating otherwise. I seem to recall one infamous scapegoater who once occupied the White House pontificate, "What you're seeing and what you're reading is not what's happening."

At the crime scene, the officers who engaged with Floyd used his "demon-possession" to scapegoat him not realizing their own demon-possession, yet everybody else present could clearly see the injustice of their treatment of a human being. The officers saw an uncontrollable menace to society while the bystanders, the former employee at the store, the paramedics, the medical staff at the hospital, and all other groups saw and affirmed the man that was George Floyd. This disparity in some ways aligns with comparing the thought process of the mob who arrest Jesus and after Jesus' trial cry out "crucify him," with those who had cried, "Hosanna, Blessed is he who comes in the name of the Lord!" as Jesus made His triumphant entry into Jerusalem just a few days before. The volatility of Black life is such that one can be honored, revered, and celebrated, and then suddenly, without warning, brutalized, callously violated, and viciously dehumanized.

As I stated before, Michelle Alexander in her classic work, *The New Jim Crow* spells out in meticulous details all the ways the criminal justice system comprehensively scapegoats brown and black bodies, I have merely touched on a few that occurred in the trial against Derek Chauvin. The tremendous pressure to find black and brown bodies guilty no matter what the cost in America's criminal justice system, is analogous to the pressure Pilate felt to find Jesus guilty, even though the gospels have Pilate declare Jesus innocent not once but twice! The salacious allegations against Jesus also coincide with the outrageous allegations against George Floyd being a threat. If I were to paint a comparison of the verdict condemning of Jesus in the gospels, with the verdicts of the court of public opinion regarding how police use qualified immunity to violently scapegoat, one could see that the common denominator on both sides is this sense of being characterized as guilty is insurmountable regardless of what evidence or truth has to say in the matter. In this way, God's Word doesn't just speak to the unique scapegoating that resulted in George Floyd's murder at the hands of police officers, the Bible speaks to how man-made governments can function as agents that sanction brutalization and oppression of select sectors of the populace when it is deemed necessary.

Since the video of George Floyd's murder was released, through the trial of the police officers involved, the supporters of white supremacy feverishly working behind the scenes, stoking the flames of demonization, in an effort to get the court of public opinion to exonerate Derek Chauvin (as well as the other officers) and sanction the concrete lynching of George Floyd, much like the Jewish leadership incited the crowd to demand that Pilate let (Jesus) Barabbas, a known insurrectionist go, but crucify Jesus the Christ. Fortunately, in this case, God has orchestrated a *Kairos* moment, and the wheels of justice are turning. The guilty verdict was evidence that David is still capable, even in an unfair fight, to slay modern-day Goliaths. More than that, ever-increasing numbers of folks who couldn't see the pervasiveness of racism before, now realize that the system as currently constructed is corrupted. There is a manufacture defect that can no longer be denied. This is not one officer or a few bad apples in a cart . . . it's the whole orchid, it's a virus embedded in the very DNA of America's existence and finally, after thousands, probably hundreds of thousands if not more black and brown bodies were victimized, those who thought we were high for saying systemic racism is alive and well and is as American as apple pie, saw George Floyd's murder, watched the trial of Derek Chauvin, rejected the false narratives the defense lawyers tried to formulate and now understand that Michael Eric Dyson is right: a reckoning with (the issue of) race in America is a "Long Time Coming."

The way in which Jesus chooses to engage (from few words to practically silence) with Caiaphas, Annas, Pilate, Herod, and then Pilate (again), shifting significantly from His combative strategy of oral confrontation with the Pharisees throughout His ministry, is another infliction point which seems to further illuminate Jesus' desire to resonate with the scapegoating of black and brown bodies approximately 2000 years later. Jesus becomes withdrawn in the judicial proceedings He is forced to go through, as if He understands and has accepted that the system is rigged against Him and He is not resisting the very fate He purposed to embrace from the very beginning. His silence prophecies the muting of the voices of all the black and brown bodies who have been silenced in their victimization as scapegoats. It was liberating to see, however, that in the case of Derek Chauvin, the indirect charges against George Floyd that the defense attempted to use to justify scapegoating George Floyd failed.

This failure is encapsulated in scripture when Pilate proclaims that both he and Herod conclude that Jesus is not guilty of the charges brought against Him, "Indeed he has done nothing to deserve death (Luke 23:15)." Was George Floyd a saint, meaning perfect? No. Each and every one of us has our faults and shortcomings, but the Word of God foretold over 2000 years ago that George Floyd did nothing to deserve death on May 25, 2020.

Connecting the Crucifixion of Jesus with the Crucifixion of George Floyd

Part of me feels it almost unnecessary to deeply examine the relationship between the crucifixion of Jesus and the concrete lynching of George Floyd. That is why this chapter is not built solely upon Jesus being scapegoated in His death. One of the purposes of this work is to emphasize the importance of showing the systemic scapegoating of Jesus from the cradle to the cross and to show how it foretells the systemic scapegoating black and brown people endure from the cradle to the grave. This seminal chapter has attempted to singularly accomplish that purpose, but the preacher in me cannot neglect the opportunity to finish the job. We must deal with how key details within the execution of Jesus inform details within communal scapegoating which then informs the violent scapegoating unarmed black men and women receive from law enforcement today.

The way in which Roman crucifixions functioned in antiquity is analogous to the function of lynching during the late 19th century in America and the function of murdering many unarmed black men and women, including George Floyd on Memorial Day, 2020. For evidence, let us begin with an excerpt from Fleming Rutledge's book *The Crucifixion: Understanding the Death of Jesus Christ:*

> *Crucifixion as a means of execution in the Roman Empire had as its express purpose the elimination of victims from consideration as members of the human race. It cannot be said too strongly: that was its function . . . crucified persons were not of the same species as either the executioners or the*

> *spectators, and were therefore, not only expendable, but also deserving of* ***ritualized*** *extermination.* (My emphasis.)

And now ponder the musing of anti-lynching activist Ida B. Wells-Barnett in her classic work *Southern Horrors* from the Selected Works of Ida B. Wells-Barnett:

> *"The editorial in question was prompted by the many inhuman and fiendish lynchings of Afro-Americans which have recently taken place and was meant as a warning. Eight lynched in one week and five of them charged with rape! The thinking public will not believe freedom and education more brutalizing than slavery, the world knows that the crime of rape was unknown during four years of Civil War, when the white women of the South were at the mercy of the race which is all at once charged with being a bestial one."*

Finally, the terror of lynchings in recent history is tied to the terror of police brutality today:

> *"it's estimated that two or three blacks were lynched each week in the American South during the late 19th and early 20th centuries. Compare that to conservative reports from the FBI that, in the seven years between 2005 and 2012, a white officer used deadly force against a black person almost two times every week. A deeper analysis by the Malcolm X Grassroots Movement found that, in just 2012, police killed more than 313 black people—one every 28 hours. MXGM also found that 44% of those killed were unarmed and 43% were not in the process of committing a crime but stopped by police for "suspicious activity."*

Roman crucifixions, the lynching of thousands of blacks in the 19th–20th centuries, and the incessant police killing of unarmed black people over the last 40 years all send the same message of dehumanizing the victim and creating irreparable separation between the scapegoat and the rest of the community. Under Roman rule, the justification was to cleanse the community of perpetrators of sedition or treason, under American ethos in the late 19–20 centuries, one of the narratives to justify lynching was to counter the fear of black men raping white women, and since the crack epidemic of the 80s, the narrative sold to the public was that police brutality was justified to keep super-predators from inflicting harm in our communities. These flimsy rationalizations coincide with the justification that killing a goat, putting blood from the goat on Joseph's coat and selling their brother into slavery was necessary in order to stop Jacob from favoring Joseph over his other sons in Genesis 37.

The scapegoating of Isaiah's Suffering Servant and the New Testament gospels reveal how violence is the tool of choice for the penalty of wrongdoing not just of the individual, but the community the individual represents. From the mindset of those who inflict the violence, it is necessary to counteract the harm from the sins committed. In lynching, the victim carries not just the weight of his or her wrongdoing (often no wrongdoing at all), but the evil the community embodies (i.e., the "narrative" of black men raping white women, or the overrepresentation of crime in poverty-stricken neighborhoods).

Finally, the visceral, brutality of Roman crucifixions, public lynching of black men and women in the late 19th century through the mid-20th century, and the murder of unarmed black bodies like George Floyd are orchestrated to intentionally inflict terror. Qualified immunity has become a shield for police officers to wield state-sponsored domestic terrorism. All they need to say is, I feared for my life, or they resisted arrest, and they have cover to dehumanize and scapegoat. What threat was George Floyd, whose hands were handcuffed behind his back, lying face down on the concrete with four officers immobilizing him, one with his knee crushing the windpipe of George Floyd? Nothing in Derek Chauvin's demeanor, nor the behavior of the other officers depicted officers fearing for their lives, but instead full of conviction. A coordinated coalition, fully persuaded to dehumanize George Floyd, because apparently, Floyd's existence was a threat to the community; apparently, he was ordained to carry the wickedness of all the criminality Chauvin had been battling. Apparently, Chauvin wanted to use the moment to send a message to the community and to his fellow officers who had much less experience than he did, that the badge gives them the right to purge and execute, cleanse and exterminate.

We have mentioned the multiple video recordings of this particular murder, and how what was seen on them caused a paradigm shift in the hearts and minds of many who now see the wretchedness of our failed experiment called democracy like never before. Ironically in scripture this same paradigm shift occurs when those who eyes were opened to the suffering of the scapegoated, discovered something they hadn't realized before. We've already discussed how the servant nations in Isaiah 53 had an awakening in their perspective of the Suffering Servant's humanity and dignity, now let us turn to the sights at Calvary.

In the Sermon "A Victorious Defeat," preached at Family of Faith A.M.E. Church, St. Thomas, USVI, on April 25, 2021, I juxtaposed what the centurion sees when he witnesses his own soldiers violently scapegoating Jesus at the cross in Luke 23:44-47, with what Minneapolis Police Chief Medaria Arrondondo saw when he witnessed a cell phone recording of his own police officers brutally scapegoating George Floyd in the street.

44 It was now about noon, and darkness came over the whole land until three in the afternoon, 45 while the sun's light failed; and the curtain of the temple was torn in two. 46 Then Jesus, crying with a loud voice, said, "Father, into your hands I commend my spirit." Having said this, he breathed his last. 47 When the centurion saw what had taken place, he praised God and said, "Certainly this man was innocent."

Whenever there was a crucifixion, one centurion was tasked with confirming to Roman leadership that the prisoner being executed died. Given the centurions' role as enforcer of Roman law and the real possibility that this centurion helped supervise the soldiers who conducted the three crucifixions at Calvary, it is no stretch to see him and his cohort functioning as police officers with the centurion acting as their "chief." The language of Luke's gospel is written such that it is what the centurion sees with his own eyes that compels him to proclaim Jesus' innocence. Similarly, the chief "centurion" of the Minneapolis Police Department, who was initially told that George Floyd had a medical emergency and who had received a narrative that conveniently neglected to mention how the officers had violated and murdered George Floyd—when Chief Medaria Arrondondo saw what had happened with his own eyes, like the centurion of scripture, he knew without a doubt Floyd was innocent of deserving the mistreatment he received from the officers under his command.

I need to underscore that the audio from those recordings is as equally gut-wrenching as the visuals. Hearing the final series of cries and pleas, moans and groans of George Floyd, is excruciatingly painful, not unlike the way our ears can't stand hearing fingernails dragged along a chalkboard. The sound of agony is harrowing, and it is no surprise that the statements of George Floyd as he fought and then finally succumbed to life leaving his body align with the statements of one whom we call the Lamb of God, as He hung on the cross in affliction on a hill called Golgotha over 2000 years ago. Michael Eric Dyson, in his important work *Long Time Coming*, and John Thomas, Editor for *The Christian Recorder*, the official newspaper of the African Methodist Episcopal Church and the oldest continuously published African-American periodical in the United States, both recognized and commemorated seven of the last statements of George Floyd, and highlight how they point rearward to and align with the seven Last Words of Jesus on the cross.

Let me be clear, I am not attempting to make an analogy between George Floyd and Jesus. I am drawing a compelling connection between the mode, the motive, and the message of Roman crucifixions, public lynching of black bodies in the late 19th through the early 20th century, and the public murder of George Floyd, recorded on a cell phone before going viral on social media. The perpetrators of violent scapegoating in each period of history shared the same ethos, using communal, state-sponsored violence for the same function, to carry out the goal of inciting fear to create a deterrent for future threats.

Whereas Bonaventure uses the power of imagination in his writings to help Jesus' followers fully comprehend/resonate with and enter into Christ's suffering, the horrid legacy of the use of excessive force by police officers, situated within a comprehensive cultural rubric of communal violent scapegoating of black and brown bodies over the past 400 plus years, means that black people don't need to stretch their imagination to understand and identify with Christ's suffering. The combination of these two realities, the nature of the suffering and the redemptive impact as a result of the sacrificial suffering is for me what links the nature of scapegoating, the Suffering Servant motif, and the death of George

Floyd (along with a host of others whose unjust killing opened the eyes of the privileged to see their own responsibility). I can already hear some folks who will be tempted to characterize this as some wild attempt to compare George Floyd to Jesus. To the true Christian, Jesus is the greatest scapegoat/lamb in history. And His legacy has spawned legions of followers who like Him, willfully decided to become suffering servants and lambs, intentionally living their lives in such a way that they embraced imitating the suffering of Jesus. This intentional embracing of suffering is emblematic of what I think is key to martyrdom. But I also believe that in the same way evil crafted the violent and communal scapegoating of Jesus yet God reconstituted Jesus' execution to redeem the world, the devil's addiction to violently scapegoating unarmed black and brown bodies compels God to reconstitute these murders to open the eyes of the privileged to see the truth. That reappropriation of power is the heart of lamb theology. The 6'4" 223 lbs. black man appeared more lion than lamb, but the video that went viral showed a gentle giant, triggered by police brandishing a gun merely seconds after tapping on the driver's side window, and terrified of getting in the back seat of a squad car with his hands handcuffed behind his back. While helpless on the ground, the gentle giant becomes the lamb that exposed the addiction to power, the co-opting of an agenda to keep black bodies subjugated, the addiction to using violent scapegoating as the means to execute the agenda of white supremacists. Unlike Jesus, George Floyd didn't choose his death, but the victory of exposing the truth, eviscerating the blue wall such that multiple representatives in law enforcement in Minneapolis and across the country publicly condemned Derek Chauvin's actions, they served as evidence of an oppressed, despised scapegoat transforming into a victorious lamb. There is only one Messiah, whose perfect example we can never reproduce, but God has chosen that despite the systemic perversion of justice resulting from black bodies being scapegoated, every now and again the Sovereign Almighty creates *Kairos* moments in time, whereby satan's ungodly agenda gets subverted and upended through the very tactics it orchestrates.

CHAPTER 6

A Tribute to Rene Girard: The Discoverer of the Scapegoat Mechanism

After watching George Floyd's murder, I demanded that God answer the question why, and God gave me one word: scapegoat. It is from there, that I uncovered scapegoating as a prominent theme throughout the Bible, and upon doing extra-biblical research, eventually stumbled onto the works of Rene Girard. His understanding of the universal nature of violence in humanity profoundly influences how I envision the dynamics of police brutality and how appealing to morality grounded in integrity may be humanity's best shot at taming violence in society.

Girard was a philosopher of human nature who was born in 1923 in Avignon, France and died in 2015. In 1947, he emigrated to America to pursue doctoral studies, and after getting his PhD from Indiana University, he stayed in America and began teaching courses on European literature. One of the famous novelists Girard studied was Dostoyevsky, and as he researched the religious conversions of some of Dostoyevsky's characters, he felt he had lived a similar experience, so he converted to Christianity. It is his Christian faith that informed his interest in ancient and contemporary sacrifice rituals, and among the myriad of literary works Girard published, I will limit the scope of this work to two of the most relevant publications, the first of which is *La Violence et le Sacré* (1972). *Violence and the Sacred* attempts to get at the fundamental element of human nature, and for Girard, it centers around notions of desire. In chapter one of this important work, he slowly flushes out a theoretical framework based on the foundational concept of mimetic desire, or desire through imitation. When we think about the fall of Adam and Eve, the conflict generated between Cain and Abel, or the enmity generated between Joseph and his brothers, they all center around mimetic desire: the serpent dangles the carrot that fuels the temptation to imitate, "God knows that when you eat of it your eyes will be opened, *and you will be like God* (italics added for emphasis), knowing good and evil" (Genesis 3:5). Murderous desire was generated by Cain for his brother Abel, built on jealousy of Abel's ability to have his sacrifice honored. To drive the point home God warns Cain about his mimetics, ". . . and if you do not do well, sin is lurking at the door, its desire is for you, but you must master it" (Genesis 4:7). And finally, sibling rivalry that ultimately became violent was built because Jacob, a father, favored one son over all the others, "But when his brothers saw that their father loved him more than all his brothers, they hated him, and could not speak peaceably to him" (Genesis 37:4). I do not hardly think that it is a coincidence that humanity's fall from grace from the very outset was baked in mimetic desire.

Girard believes that sometimes the rivalry which showcases the desire is over something or someone external, but as the desire evolves, often is not about the object or the external person, but about the relationship between the rival and what Girard calls the model. Transfixing desire from the object to the model, creates the conditions for irrational thought to become tempting as violence seems to be a way to tame desire. Thus, Girard's theory sheds light on explaining the cyclical nature of violence by describing how initially a rival desires to possess what the model possesses, then ultimately shifts from wanting the object the model wants, to wanting to be the model. According to Girard, the desire becomes all-consuming, tricking the brain into hallucinating that the best way to satiate the desire is by violence, which temporarily creates a false equilibrium. However, the loved ones of the victim of the violence are not in equilibrium, so they lash out to imitate the murderous rival who has now become the model, and the cycle continues. "Mimetic desire is, according to Girard, the primary impulse of living creatures. Accordingly, the violence that such desire inevitably engenders is an almost inescapable facet of human society. Left unchecked, the mimetic impulse leads to violence and murder under the pretense that the violence will lead to homeostasis. Unfortunately, this sense of stability is a myth as murder ultimately leads to another murder and thus to the beginning of an unstoppable chain of reciprocal violence and vengeance which threatens to destroy the entire community. This period of chaotic violence is termed the sacrificial crisis." Now we have come full circle in understanding why this classic work is entitled *Violence and the Sacred.*

When I apply Girard's lens of mimetic theory to the ongoing, wicked phenomenon called police brutality, elements of it make some sense. The men and women in blue, not having exorcised themselves fully from the wretchedness of their beginnings as slave catchers, are agents of white supremacy, put in place to make sure black and brown bodies never experience total independence, never attain complete and total liberation from white control. For the sake of maintaining social order, the state sanctions violence against the imitators, deeming them not worthy of attaining independence from white control because it threatens their conceptualization of a civil society. The mission to maintain a civil society becomes a sacred, crusade-like responsibility that appears to embrace a noble goal. Therefore, the mentality of inflicting violence to create or sustain a sense of the sacred grows stronger and stronger until acted upon.

This is the double conundrum of police brutality . . . it will take Herculean efforts to reverse engineer the state-sponsored communal violence of black and brown bodies because, according to Girard, it is the violence itself that facilitates access to the sacred, where true community can be restored. If nothing else, mimetic theory helps us understand the perniciousness of violence against black and brown people. And until we can rid violence of its false promise to the attainment of peace and reconciliation, as long as police departments take cues from the likes of Lt. Col. Dave Grossman, whose nationwide police trainings are based on a "killology ethos," blurring the lines between war "combat as a soldier in a foreign land and fighting crime on the mean streets of urban America," America will continue perpetuating the myth that brutalizing black people cleanses the community, covers a multitude of sins, and atones the community's relationship with God. Efforts that ignore this important undercurrent, no matter how well-intended, will never break the chain.

One may ask, what about the number of dead bodies that have piled up over the decades and centuries due to violence against the other? According to Girard, those bodies were sacrifices offered in ritualistic fashion to help mitigate mimetic desire and instead bring about communal peace. This explains why some people can look at Derek Chauvin and refuse to see him guilty of murdering George Floyd, or why they feel the incessant violence waged disproportionately against black and brown bodies functions on a "higher" level for the good of the community at large.

Ironically, it is not the rival who initiates violence, it is the model, who see the rival's desire for independence as a threat to their homeostasis. If we frame the mimetic desire as achieving autonomy void of external control, the more the marginalized fight to achieve what the autonomous white supremacists have achieved, and the more the white supremacists both demonize and deify the marginalized. The marginalized are demonized because they are rivals threatening to obtain independence from white control which would upend white supremacy. But the marginalized at the same time also function as sacred and priceless, uniquely qualified to be used as sacrifice on behalf of attaining peace for the community. How else could the community thrive if it didn't have a healthy supply of those called to sacrifice themselves, for the greater good of society?

The irony of *Violence and the Sacred* is that Girard puts forth this notion that the oppressors never overtly signal their intentions to sacrifice the marginalized, they exploit a misunderstanding to justify the need for sacrifice while at the same time not recognizing the violence inflicted upon others as sacrifice. This misunderstanding within the framework of police brutality is the cover of law and order. In other words, for years police departments successfully sold to the public that having cops bend the rules, ignore protocols, act as judge, jury, and executioner on the streets with little to no accountability is an acceptable means to the end of having thriving communities, safe from criminal activities. Therefore, Girard argues, religion was invented in the form of a supernatural being demanding the sacrifice. In most societies, animal sacrifice became a substitute for human sacrifice. However, if the catharsis of animal sacrifice was not enough to maintain a society, then human sacrifice was employed. The culture that arises from this religious impulse will have sacrificial ritual, myth, and prohibitions. Girard sees the Old Testament characters,

Abel and Joseph, functioning in mimetic rivalry, as agents of sacrifice, and in each case, Girard sees misunderstanding by the violators as the conduit that promotes violence.

"What this mimetic desire means is that it is not the differences between the various members of a community that brings about violence, but rather the erosion of those differences: what Girard calls the 'sacrificial crisis' is the theoretical and historical event in which the cultural order, warrant of social differentiation, loses its authority. The result is the spread of violence, as one crime calls for a vengeance, and the vengeance, in turn, calls for another crime, and so on, in what he terms a deadly reciprocity."

Jesus' example of resisting violence is actualized when we desire the life offered to us by God be offered to others in turn. Jesus' refusal to enact violence on those who had acted against Him short-circuits the cycle of violence and removes the need for the mechanism of the sacrificial victim. When black and brown bodies have ceased to be objectified as targeted rivals, humanity has the opportunity to pattern our desires after the desires of Christ and break the cycle of violence.

In describing *Violence and the Sacred*, I have intentionally avoided the use of the term scapegoat, because, in 1986, Girard published *The Scapegoat,* regarded as one of the most important works written on the intersection of culture, violence and religion. From the persecution of Jews in mid-14th century France to the origins of the Meso-American myth of Teotihuacan, to the role the Paraclete plays in facilitating the bridge between the world and the Divine, Rene Girard's *The Scapegoat* is fifteen chapters of passionately relating his theory of mimesis to the origin of mythology, featuring the collective murder of a scapegoat. Prior to *The Scapegoat*, Girard touched on the notion that the scapegoat mechanism is found in historical events and throughout important historical books, but in this work, Girard devotes much of his psychoanalysis of culture, religion, and violence to the Passion of Jesus Christ.

In this way, it would seem that years ago, as I adopted this notion that the Bible is uniquely qualified to illuminate diverse aspects of human nature and can inspire us to be better versions of ourselves, discovering *The Scapegoat* confirmed my calling (as part of my journey to understand the violent phenomena of police brutality) as it bore witness to how the gospels flush out communal scapegoating. Girard recounting real-life history and abstract mythologies to analyze patterns of scapegoating throughout is grandiose in scope, but practically all critics acknowledge that Girard definitely is onto something, even if they balk at calling his claim of the scapegoat mechanism being universally definitive. On the other hand, the massacres of Jews that occurred in France and elsewhere in Europe during the plague years were examples of collective violence against innocent victims, singled out in a time of crisis to serve as scapegoats. Girard uses this account of a historical event combined with poetic embellishment told through the lens of a persecutor to flush out what he calls the four stereotypes of the scapegoat mechanism. "The first stereotype is the description of a social and cultural crisis which results in a generalized loss of differences. The second is the crime that eliminates differences. The third is that those perceived to have committed these crimes possess the marks of a victim. The fourth is the violence itself." Girard then applies these stereotypes to meticulous readings of myths, ranging from the story of Oedipus to myths of the Dogrib (from northwest Canada), the Aztecs, and the Scandinavian peoples.

Girard uses specific narratives of both historical events and myths to craft a cohesive hypothesis that our wants and desires are shaped entirely by imitation of those closest to us and those we commend. It is this desire to imitate that pulls us into competition, which leads to conflict and left unchecked, leads to violent scapegoating. And yet, the scapegoaters unconsciously hallucinate about the nature of the violence by creating a mythical narrative regarding the guilt of the victim. "The way to assure that scapegoats are not recognized as what they really are is by distorting the story of the events that led to their death. This is accomplished by telling the story from the perspective of the scapegoaters. Myths will usually tell a story of someone doing a terrible thing and, thus, deserving to be punished. The victim's perspective will never be incorporated into the myth, precisely because this would spoil the psychological effect of the scapegoating mechanism. The victim will always be portrayed as a culprit whose deeds brought about social chaos, but whose death or expulsion brought about social peace."

While I remain unconvinced that mimetic desire is able to explain and is at the root of all conflicts that lead to violence, Girard's theory of human culture and its propensity to observe how proponents of violence fraudulently frame scapegoating as a means to obtain peace is compelling. When I attempt to appropriate Girard's mimetic desire to the violence of police brutality against black and brown bodies, I'm straining to discover mimesis; neither is trying to imitate the other. Can I envision contexts where imitation breeds violence? Undoubtedly! But I just can't discern how it applies in the world of police using excessive force on select, unarmed "persons of interest." This is where I agree with some of Girard's critics who contend that Girard is feeling himself more than he should when he dares to posit that his mimetic theory is at the core of all violence.

On the other hand, his flushing out of the scapegoat mechanism as he refers to it, absolutely sheds significant light on the why of police brutality in America. The seemingly incessant addiction some police officers have about seeing black and brown bodies as worthy of abuse in ways they would never treat those who have been deemed privileged makes sense if these agents of law enforcement are operating (inadvertently) from the framework of the violence as covering (a multitude of sins), wiping/purging, redeeming, to sacrifice/appease (seeking favor from God). It explains its persistence despite the growing awareness of its immorality. I believe the purpose of police brutality generating communal peace was present at the very outset of police departments, designated as Slave Patrols in the early 18th century in the South. One of the primary functions of these patrols was to maintain a form of discipline for slave workers who were subject to summary justice, outside of the law, if they violated any plantation rules. The summary justice served to both instill terror to deter slave revolts and to restore peace among the white supremacists who rightfully saw runaway slaves a threat to their system of white control.

Thus, the violence inflicted by the slave owners as told from their perspective, operates within Girard's scapegoat mechanism as they transfer their own sin born out of the need to prevent the collapse of social order, to maintain power through the operationalization of systemic racism onto innocent victims, who are (mis)characterized as egregious lawbreakers deserving to be punished. Furthermore, "Girard believes that, as myths evolve, later versions will tend to dissimulate the scapegoating violence (for example, instead of presenting a victim who dies by drowning, the myth will just claim that the victim went to live to the bottom of the sea), in order to avoid feeling compassion for the victim." The resurgence of downplaying the role of slavery in American history, the revisionist narratives of the intent of the Three-Fifths Compromise as somehow helping to mitigate the power of Southern states, and the minimizing of the violence against our democracy on January 6th, 2021 are all gross attempts to downplay the significance of the violence of the scapegoaters that certain politicians are attempting to minimize and reappropriate as historical fact.

While *The Scapegoat* mines through historical events and myths to validate Girard's hypothesis about mimetic theory triggering the scapegoat mechanism, when he turns to the Bible, and the gospels in particular, to his delight, the point of reference for the unfolding of the narration shifts from the perspective of the scapegoaters to the perspective of the victims. "However, according to Girard, this is not merely a shift in narrative perspective. It is in fact something much more profound. Inasmuch as the Bible presents stories from the perspective of the victims, the Biblical authors reveal something not understood by previous mythological traditions. And, by doing so, they make scapegoating inoperative. Once scapegoats are recognized for what they truly are, the scapegoating mechanism no longer works. Thus, the Bible is a remarkably subversive text, inasmuch as it shatters the scapegoating foundations of culture." Whereas the perpetrators of violence are wildly disillusioned in the way they frame the violence, the victims give an account of the scapegoating from a completely different lens, and in so doing, show how compelling Girard's interpretative analysis is in explaining human nature. "Girard contends that the Christian Bible, the combination of the Old and New Testaments, has provided that force of revelation" which enables readers in the twentieth century (and beyond) to recognize persecution texts for what they are. Thus, although 'human culture is predisposed to the permanent concealment of its origins in collective violence,' Girard is hopeful."

To extrapolate Girard's analysis to the murder of George Floyd is to see Floyd's victimization via violent scapegoating on a metaphysical level, transcending our physical reality. This work is grounded in the belief that God's Word provides distinct insights about how a human being could press their knee on an unarmed person's neck for nine and a half minutes and it make perfect sense. It is my hope that in some way, this publication has made us even more confident of the ability of God's Word to speak profoundly to current circumstances. But what *Violence and the Sacred* as well as *The Scapegoat* have shown us through the genius of Rene Girard, is that police officers, in their seemingly intractable allegiance to violent scapegoating of black and brown bodies, are participating in something much more than physical violence. To apply Girard's scapegoat mechanism to police brutality is to recognize its function as sacred ritual. To frame it as such seems strange, until we recall how the bastion of white supremacy groups, the KKK, weaved together narratives about violence, scapegoating and the sacred in the burning cross. In other words, the burning cross for the KKK symbolizes the intersection of holy sacrifice, and violent scapegoating. To Girard's point, the Bible uses the cross of Calvary to shed light on the voice of the victims of scapegoating, whereas the KKK used the burning cross to create a narrative from the voice of the scapegoater. Listen to the voice of the scapegoater and how Bob Jones, one of the KKK's most iconic leaders in history frame the violence in the language of sacred ritual: the burning cross is a "'symbol of sacrifice and service, and a sign of the Christian Religion sanctified and made holy nearly 19 centuries ago, by the suffering and blood of 50 million martyrs who died in the most holy faith.'" "He emphasized cross burnings as 'driv[ing] away darkness and gloom . . . by the fire of the Cross we mean to purify and cleanse our virtues by the fire on His Sword.' Such grandiose rhetoric, of course, could not dispel the reality that the KKK frequently deployed burning crosses as a means of terror and intimidation, and also as a spectacle to draw supporters and curious onlookers to their nightly rallies, which always climaxed with the *ritualized* burning of a cross that often extended 60 or 70 feet into the sky."

KKK scholar David Cunningham notes that the "KKK's emphasis on violence and intimidation as a means to defend its white supremacist ends has been the primary constant across its various 'waves.' . . . Indeed, in the absence of the group's association with violence and terror, the Klan's emphasis *on secrecy and ritual* would have lost much of its nefarious mystique, but KKK-style lawlessness frequently went hand-in-hand with corruption among its own leaders. More importantly, Klan violence also often resulted in a backlash against the group, both from authorities and among the broader public."

The KKK's weaving of violent scapegoating with sacred ritual to further the agenda of white supremacy is significant, and even more noteworthy given the reality that serving as agents of racist ideology, they intentionally infiltrated law enforcement groups. "In 2006, the bureau compiled an intelligence report concerning a growing threat to the country's police departments. Entitled 'White Supremacist Infiltration of Law Enforcement,' it warned of right-wing extremists' efforts to join the ranks of local police forces. 'White supremacist leaders and groups,' it states, 'have historically shown an interest in infiltrating law enforcement or recruiting law enforcement personnel.'" When we put all the data together, we can recognize that police brutality historically has functioned as sacred ritual, and for me, that revelation completely transforms how we ought to envision the violence as well as how we as a national and global community need to confront it.

Another way Girard's analysis of scapegoating in the Bible is enlightening if not instructive to the dynamics of George Floyd's murder, is that, like the scapegoating of Jesus in the gospel, an undeniable narrative from the "faces at bottom of the well" emerges. Just as the gospels subvert the perspective of the scapegoaters who violate Jesus, the violence waged against George Floyd became subversive in that it blew a hole into the seemingly invincible blue wall and allowed the victim's viewpoint to shine. The attempts of the scapegoaters to have their frame of reference dominate the narrative epically failed, and the trial allowed the voice and view of the victims (when you include the bystanders) to prevail. Instead, the lynching/crucifixion revived and reenergized a movement that to this day, still has formidable momentum to create the conditions for comprehensive police reform. *The Scapegoat* underscores Girard's belief that the gospels both reveal the nature of human beings and the nature of God. I would contend that especially in this *Kairos* moment in history, part of what justice looks like is being privileged to be exposed to this dual phenomenon, where the uncovering of police brutality functioning as sacred ritual exposes humanity's penchant towards self-destruction, but at the same time, God manifests a window of opportunity in the midst of (and in spite of) the violence for redemption.

When we push Girard's analysis harder, we reimagine what Christ's suffering really means for humanity. Traditionally, Christ's death is seen as an act of vicarious atonement, necessary to satisfy the Father's unalterable demand for the punishment of sin. In contrast, Girard argues that Christ's death marked the *rejection* of sacrifice—and thus (rejection also) of the perennial legitimization of violence. Under Girard's interpretation, Jesus saved us by becoming a victim and overturning once and for all the scapegoat mechanism. Thanks to Jesus' salvific mission, human beings now have the capacity to understand what scapegoats really are and have the golden opportunity to achieve enduring social peace. The intensive study of *The Scapegoat* leads not only to an exercise of the intellect but also to the discovery of a universal self-deluding pattern of human thought and behavior which, once identified, will be a step toward ending human violence.

CHAPTER 7

Where Do We Go from Here?

The scapegoat mechanism as flushed out in this book has focused on tying the violence inflicted upon George Floyd, through the scapegoating of Jesus, all the way back to the scapegoating of Joseph and a literal goat by Joseph's brothers in Genesis. I have focused on how this political mechanism was implemented by Joseph's brothers to violate him, reappropriated by divine law for righteousness in Leviticus 16, re-weaponized and wielded upon the Suffering Servant in Isaiah 53, incorporated by the religious aristocracy in antiquity to criminalize and demonize Jesus, and in America, institutionalized by law enforcement to permanently subjugate the masses of black and brown people globally. In America, the scapegoat mechanism has functioned to deny black people access to comprehensive independence outside the bounds of white supremacy. As George Floyd's murder has shown, the scapegoat mechanism also has served as a tool to sanction violence against individuals who otherwise pose no impending, imminently fatal threat to society. In fact, our preeminent public intellectuals, Drs. Cornel West and Michael Eric Dyson have both opined that the persistence of state-sanctioned communal violence is a threat to our democracy in America. ". . . even white folk cannot truly enjoy the benefits of race, or the democracy on which they are supposed to rest, unless all of us, ultimately, are free." ". . . here we are in 2021 saying . . . do we have what it takes to acknowledge the rich humanity of black folk, to treat us fairly, to treat us like human beings, because if not, you're going to lose your democracy."

Seeing the recording of the murder of George Floyd for me, and I am confident for many people globally, was existential. It was groundbreaking not because we hadn't seen violent scapegoating in the form of police brutality against black and brown bodies previously, but because God through this victim who was innocent of deserving death that day, showed me how to view police brutality in a way I hadn't previously. Witnessing people from all over the world react and respond to the murder the way they did, rejecting the usual criminalization and demonization of the victim which is almost unprecedented when the scapegoat is black, cemented for me the need to understand how God's Word, in particular, makes sense out of this *Kairos* moment in history.

If God hadn't used Darnella Frazier, motivating the 17-year-old young woman to record the 10-minute execution of George Floyd, many people would still be in denial about the grossly disproportionate use of excessive force by police officers. Just to emphasize how critical Ms. Frazier's video was to facilitate this *Kairos* moment, the original police description of George Floyd's death (based largely on the fact that Derek Chauvin neglected to tell his superiors of the nine-minute, twenty-nine-second chokehold he "administered,") was "Man Dies After Medical Incident During Police Interaction." Unlike other bystanders who expressed their guilt for not being able to help, and unlike the other three officers, who went along with Derek Chauvin's agenda, Ms. Frazier found empowering agency in the midst of menacing terror that resulted in aiding humanity to see the injustice interwoven into the very fabric of American police departments. We would do well to follow her lead. Not just by recording injustice when it shows its ugly face, (it has proven its power) but we also can follow her lead by grounding ourselves in our own God-given calling to exercise defiant resistance.

I cannot neglect this opportunity to link her actions to the implicit defiance shown by Jesus when violent scapegoating reached its zenith at His own crucifixion. Good Friday was good not only because it set the stage for Resurrection Sunday, but it was also good because it exposed blatant corruption by Roman (police) centurions acting at the behest of the government (and the Jewish elite) and the defiance the Son of Man showed in the face of violent terror. Just as many police officers saw and called out the inhumane treatment of George Floyd and praised God for the defeat of unjust policing on April 19, 2021, the scripture records a centurion saw Jesus' suffering and in watching His nonviolent defiance, praised God for the vindication from the violent scapegoating of Jesus. Jesus' example of resistance on the cross as narrated in John's gospel, and the power wielded by a young woman using her cell phone to record ungodly abuse of power on May 25, 2020, teach us the value of finding our calling in the midst of suffering and death. God has created a bouquet of humanity, as lead prosecutor Jerry Blackwell reminded us, and our calling is to find our own unique voice which can be coordinated with other voices to nonviolently bring down corrupt institutions. In under ten minutes, Darnella Frazier accomplished what may have taken a lifetime or more to achieve otherwise.

On the other hand, the shootings that have occurred after George Floyd's murder, from Jacob Blake to Andrew Brown Jr. and continuing, have served to remind us that despite the impact of Floyd's murder, despite the significance of Chauvin's conviction, the blue wall/empire has not been decimated; indeed, it is alive and well. The system continues to use violence as the tool of choice even in this heightened season of the need to reimagine policing.

I am grateful that God tasked me to reverse engineer how the concept of violent, ritualistic scapegoating has been a tactic used overtly and covertly during police encounters with black and brown civilians in ways that have exacted negative consequences. Moving forward, having laid this foundation, I hope to expound even further on diverse ways in which we can apply the lessons of this work to contexts not mentioned here. Now that we know better, let's work together individually and collectively to do better. The question is how? I've already mentioned the criminal justice legislative initiatives that were stewing prior to George Floyd's murder, and the numerous policy initiatives that have been introduced since. In addition to them, how can we move the needle and do policing better? For some, it means directly intervening when police officers are using excessive force, and in so doing, literally put ourselves in harm's way. While I appreciate the sentiments of my cherished professor, Dr. Cornel West, who made an indelible impression on me when I saw him preach a sermon "Legion" at Bethel A.M.E. Church in Baltimore, MD in the late 1980s, and then taught me during my senior year at Princeton Theological Seminary as I took electives at Princeton University across the street, I am empathetic to the behavior of the bystanders to not escalate an already tense situation *to a degree*. The call to aggressively confront police officers who are "licensed to kill" is a tall order, to put it modestly. Furthermore, we live in a culture of hyper-individualism such that we are trained to see most folks who are not blood relatives as nonfamily. The public is quick to judge the training of police officers, but we overlook the training needed to lean in and intervene in these kinds of life-or-death situations. At the height of the civil rights movement, organizations like SNCC provided resistance training to equip its members with evidence-based strategies for confrontations with police officers. Therefore, how can we expect people, even those who look like me and share my experience of being dehumanized in America, to see nonrelatives as family, embrace their suffering as our own, and recognize our own agency to intercede on their behalf when that is not where we are today nationally? I am very confident that there are outstanding stakeholders that have progressive programs centered around raising and training revolutionaries capable of leaning into their calling and finding agency when the terror of violent scapegoating is being waged. And yes, the church, especially the black church, and yes even more so the A.M.E. Church with its distinctive social justice DNA in-bred from its inception, should see this work as part and parcel of our calling, but that mentality is far from normative in our culture today.

And yet, those realities of a lack of resources are not reason to endorse standing on the sidelines, watch anybody slowly murder another human being, and be unwilling to break the man-made laws that would hinder us from validating George Floyd's humanity. Those realities are a searing critique of the distance between who we say we are as Christians versus who Jesus is; a revolutionary led by the Holy Spirit who often defied man-made laws to affirm the humanity of others. I cannot sit here and say that everyone who stood and watched, or who walked by and merely witnessed is indicted for failing to try to intervene. I am saying that nobody intervening is an indictment of where we are as a national community.

Imagine a Savior who got so incensed at the systemic scapegoating in the temple and the dehumanization of the vulnerable that took place in the house of God, that He defied the powerful by aggressively confronting them; at what point in our current context, do we follow *that* Jesus? How do we go about the work of breaking down scripture to reveal a God who gives us agency to respond in times like these and then teach our children, our women, and especially our men that the ongoing extermination of our brothers and sisters by police officers in plain sight—because they can hide behind qualified immunity—is unacceptable and must be confronted in a multitude of ways? At what point do we recognize that failing to follow *that* Jesus, indirectly condones and facilitates the dehumanization we so passionately want to see destroyed?

When white folk do their part, deal with their fear and insecurity around the notion of becoming a majority minority in less than 30 years and recognize that exposing and neutralizing white privilege is the only way democracy for all has a chance, we can make strides in dismantling the dynamics of violent scapegoating functioning as the tool of choice for upholding white supremacy. Many white people are coming to grips with the depth of the problem; they now understand that it is not just a bad apple here or there, but instead, America is starving for systemic change. Many have joined the movement and given of their time and energy to the cause of reimagining policing; some because they are compelled to believe what they refused to believe previously, but their eyes are showing them now. Others because they now realize that the denial of the humanity of black and brown people will sabotage the potential of the American experiment to succeed. Surely W. E. B. DuBois was correct when he said the problem of the 20th century is the color line, but an even more accurate statement is that from its inception, the American experiment has been and continues to be fatally flawed because of its dependence and addiction to using scapegoating as a tool in various forms, creating structural racism to serve the purpose of maintaining white supremacy. I believe there are some Lincoln protegees, who embrace the utilitarian approach he had about slavery dividing the union, and they now join the movement, because they have a vested interest in not wanting to see America defeat itself from within. Even if someone's motives for working toward rebuilding a new public safety system are solely tied to self-interest and not authentic compassion, George Floyd is the triumphant, sacrificial lamb who helped usher in engagement that can impact our society for good. The phrases "white privilege" and "white fragility" predate the murder of George Floyd, but their usage in American discourse has gained momentum since then, and the honest self-reflections by white people about how society coddles white fragility and how they have benefitted in a multitude of ways from white privilege could reap great dividends toward societal progress. And yet, with all that white people need to do, including having uncomfortable conversations, getting involved in campaigns for systemic change, even looking at their own biases and fears, I'm not confident that by itself, it will be enough.

When police officers do their part, recognizing the culture and training of police departments as still connected to the mentality and ethos of slave patrols functioning to recapture slaves and appease oppressive slave owners, when they stop treating protestors as enemy combatants, and instead, reimagine policing that prioritizes the balance of officer safety and the preservation of the life and dignity of all members of the community, we will be well on our way to moving the needle in the right direction. Police departments around the country are now in the spotlight to see which ones will follow Minneapolis Police Chief Medaria Arradondo's aggressive assault on the blue wall of silence in calling out the excessive force used by his officers on May 25, 2020. As much as I applaud his assistance in tearing open the blue wall of silence, it cannot be neglected to mention that former officer Chauvin's facial expression, combined with the ease of his calculated movements conveyed an officer who had been a violent scapegoater long before that fateful afternoon on African Liberation Day 2020. When we fully dissect the ramifications of this data, it means that a rogue officer was comfortable using his police uniform as a shield to conduct his vicious brutality. Since his body language indicated his ease in dehumanizing his victims, it stands to reason that there are others on that force who know, condone, and/or fully supported his mode of operation. Any attempt to try to portray Chauvin as a lone wolf that no one knew about falls on deaf ears in my book. Given the corrupt practice of police brutality that led to a longtime veteran on that force to rise to leadership, had Chief Medaria Arradondo conducted a thorough investigation to identify and neutralize the Derek Chauvins on the force when he took the helm, it potentially could have prevented George Floyd's tragedy. In the aftermath of George Floyd's death, and the continuing incidents of the use of excessive force by police officers under his watch, the community ought to pressure the Chief whether he has since employed rigorous vetting strategies to identify other officers who have the mindset and policing ethos that Chauvin had. Better recruitment mechanisms to weed out potential officers who have yet to mitigate their implicit, racist bias needs to happen. In a perfect world, police departments wouldn't need statutory mandates or scandalous incidents of police brutality to reduce police misconduct and improve public safety. Instead of waiting for consent decrees, or the passage of the George Floyd Justice in Policing Act to compel them into compliance, police departments across the board could proactively ban chokeholds, end qualified immunity, ban no-knock warrants and create more deterrence of the use of excessive force by having millions of dollars awarded annually from police misconduct lawsuits to come from the pensions of the department, not innocent taxpayers. New Testament scholar Esau McCaulley does a brilliant job of demonstrating how God's Word provides what he calls a "Theology of Policing," by linking the roles of the Roman soldiers in antiquity with the role of police officers today and incorporating the insights from his exegesis should help us change the culture of policing in America. But again, I am not confident that if all police departments enacted these measures alone, it would eradicate police brutality.

In researching for the book, I sought to get the perspective of police officers on police brutality, because it is easy to sit from a distance and quarterback what we feel they should do, when the reality is, unless we've gone through the training to become proficient in their craft, and been in those life threatening situations, we really don't know. In talking to my cousin Antonio Bascilio and one of my younger brother's best friends, D. Crockett, both of whom have experience as police officers, I now have greater appreciation for the difficult work they are called to do and not make any mistakes, because the margin of error often can cost someone their life.

My cousin, who we call Tony, stopped working for police departments in Maryland many years ago, but he hasn't forgotten the culture of policing that carries through today. When I asked him about the culture of policing, he quickly chimed in about the inception of policing in America being tied to the business of catching runaway slaves. But the one thing that he said which really stuck with me is the notion that the culture of police departments enables citizens to join the force so that they *can* (legally) *break the law*. I think in the back of many African American's minds is the fear that folks who are affiliated with white supremacist groups are attracted to the notion of becoming police officers so that they can legally actualize their desire to demonize and scapegoat black and brown bodies. For years people have dismissed these claims as false cries of desperation, but in Timeline.com's July 11, 2016 article, written by Matt Reiman, entitled "Actual White Supremacist Cops Are Hiding in Plain Sight," Larrissa Moore, a law student who has studied reams of Civil Rights-era murder records, explained how the Klan encouraged its members to infiltrate the ranks of law enforcement. This effort began as early as the 1960s, a time when social progress was weakening the Klan's ability to terrorize black lives. According to Moore, they believed that the laws wouldn't 'apply to them *if they are the law*.'

Reiman goes on to say that "in recent years, the entanglement of law enforcement and white supremacy has gotten a fair amount of press. In September (of 2015), police officer Raymond Mott was fired after a photo surfaced of him performing a Nazi salute at an anti-immigration rally. The year before, two Florida officers were fired when they were found having ties to the KKK. And in 2001, a similar story occurred when two deputies in Texas who had a strong allegiance to the Klan were dismissed. These recent cases bring to mind an infiltration strategy outlined by the FBI report called 'ghost skins,' a method in which members of white supremacist groups modulate their behavior and appearance in order to 'to blend into society and covertly advance white supremacist causes.'"

In this way, the blue wall becomes a barrier that shields men and women from prosecution who are willing to use the cover of law enforcement to exert violence on black and brown bodies. My cousin's statements as a former police officer aligned with the revelation on January 6th, active duty service members were among those who stormed the US Capitol. "At least 31 law enforcement officers across 12 states were being scrutinized by their agencies for their participation in January 6th failed insurrection in Washington, the Associated Press reported in late January. At least five current or former police officers have been charged so far in connection with the Capitol riot, according to National Public Radio. As of mid-February, at least six Capitol police officers had been suspended without pay for their behavior on January 6th, and 29 others were under investigation, according to news reports. In addition, at least 33 individuals with known military backgrounds have been charged in connection with the Capitol attack, according to George Washington University's program on extremism."

The experience of D. Crockett, who continues to serve on the police force after 15 years is quite different from my cousin Tony. Having served in multiple police departments, "D" expressed that while he has worked with many white officers over the years, he hasn't really seen the kind of overt use of excessive force in his dealings that we often see on television. We went over several police shootings from the past several months as well as George Floyd's murder, and it was instructive to get the perspective of someone who I respect and who is trained for those situations, versus me watching a video talking about could've, should've, would've. In discussing George Floyd's murder, Officer Crockett said that not being able to hear from Derek Chauvin was unfortunate because he would've liked to understand his mindset. He claimed practically every colleague he spoke with on the force agreed that Chauvin was way over the top and clearly has some issues. We then shifted to discuss Adam Toledo, the 13-year-old boy shot by police in Chicago on March 29th. I told "D" that the major problem I had with that shooting was that the young boy complied with the officer's request; he stopped, dropped his gun and he showed his hands. "D" began to share how waiting for another fraction of a second could've cost the officer his life, and that the 13-year-old boy had a nickname, Little Murder. I doubled down, insisting that regardless of what people called him, when any civilian follows a police officer's orders, the civilian should be able to see another day. I hammered home the point that following police directions should not be the cause for death, to which "D" replied that he hoped trainers would begin to retool officers to give commands that won't put the civilians in a no-win situation. Then we spoke about Daunte Wright, the young man killed less than 20 minutes away from the location where George Floyd was murdered. "D" said he believed that it was a mistake and that the trainer who yelled taser did so desiring to tase Mr. Wright, not shoot him with her gun. We went back and forth about the nature of former officer Kim Potter's multiple errors and how she contributed to the killing by intervening when the other officer was attempting to handcuff Daunte. "D" said once the officers ran his plates and found a warrant, he wasn't going to get out of being arrested, but I questioned the racial profiling technique of pulling someone over a person of color simply for having air fresheners hang from their mirror. Lastly, we discussed Ma'kia Bryant, who was shot by a police officer on the same day as the George Floyd verdict. Again, we went back and forth about the various details of the case, and with each factor, "D" expressed the weakness of alternative, non-lethal strategies, and noted how the officer's bodycam footage showed the victim poised to stab another girl, who was pinned against the car with nowhere to go. "D" said the officer did exactly what he was trained to do, and if he was in the same circumstances, he believed he would've done the same thing. Ironically, in checking on my Facebook page, another friend, who happens to be a black, retired police officer, and a minister, basically stated the same thing; the officer did exactly what he was trained to do at that moment.

Going through each of these scenarios with "D" helped me to realize how incredibly nuanced each one is, and I began to wrap my head around the reality that being a black police officer made an already hard occupation to master, significantly more difficult. "D" shared that he feels black cops are more at risk than any other demographic simply because the community often considers him a sellout and as anti-community simply because of the profession he chose. The two-hour engagement I had with "D" didn't necessarily change our minds about how we see these deadly incidents, but it broadened our perspectives and helped each of us see that forming opinions based on one perspective does a disservice to the overarching goal; reimagining police so that black and brown bodies cease from being disproportionately violated. I am confident he came away recognizing that policing can no longer unequivocally prioritize officer safety over and above the need for citizens to be able to trust that law enforcement will revert to the use of significant force only when it is absolutely necessary. The quest to reimagine policing must create realities where those two dynamics are not competing against each other but working in tandem with each other. The Adam Toledo shooting is relevant here in that the officer could have given a set of commands to the young boy which provided a means for him to show the officer his intent to surrender, comply and face due process, but from what I've seen, the officer apparently failed to create that opportunity, which validates the lack of trust certain communities have toward police officers.

I know "D" personally, having watched him grow up with my brother for the past 40 plus years. I know his heart and I know his love of God and his agenda to want to serve his community faithfully. When we discussed the George Floyd murder, and the role Thomas Lane, J. Alexander Keung and Tou Thao played, he explained to me that the culture of the blue wall makes it impossible for newbies to not follow the lead of senior officers. "D" mentioned the "initiation" newbies go through, not unlike that which is found in fraternities and sororities. This reminded me of the courage of Cariol Horne, a former Buffalo police officer fired for preventing her partner from violently choking a suspect. Earlier this year, the courts vindicated Horner, giving her backpay and pension, with Erie County Supreme Court Judge Dennis E. Ward referencing the cases of George Floyd and Eric Garner—the New York man who died after being placed in a chokehold—among other alleged instances of excessive force by police. One can only hope that Buffalo's Cariol Law, which obligates officers to intervene and seeks to legally protect those who do, will catch fire across the nation. "D" also spoke in detail about two separate incidents where he intervened to de-escalate and prevent white officers who were about to cross the line with their use of force. He informed me that while acknowledging the disparity between how blacks are treated versus how whites in similar situations are treated by law enforcement officers, the media doesn't show that in many other scenarios, white suspects are assaulted and get shot, as well as circumstances where blacks are confronted by white officers affirming their humanity and dignity even in hostile situations.

When I first heard these comments, I understood why many in the black community call black police officers sellouts, but knowing "D" personally compelled me to see why "D" is intentional about seeing these incidents from multiple perspectives. As a black Christian living in a US territory where some may see my faith as adopting the white man's religion, I am passionate about shattering preconceived notions others have about Christianity and the Bible's relevance for the empowerment of people who look like me. As a pastor in the African Methodist Episcopal Church, I align with the notion of wanting to defend being a part of a mainline protestant denomination that uses the term African as part of its moniker. As a divorced pastor, I resonate with the desire to challenge others to broaden their vista and envision reality from multiple perspectives.

When I reflected deeply about "D" and his service to the community as a police officer, it reminded me that all of us situate ourselves in groups and organizations that carry with them distinct narratives, and whether those narratives are accurate or not, they don't tell the whole story and we cannot blindly appropriate those narratives to any one individual. Reinhold Niebuhr in his classic work, *Moral Man, Immoral Society*, masterfully analyzes how group dynamics subliminally influence and affect individual behavior and thinking. All of us belong to groups and organizations which we try to influence, and which inevitably influence us. Though we didn't always see eye to eye on each scenario, and that is not necessarily a bad thing, I was proud to hear "D" struggle to maintain his own individuality and push back against institutional norms within police departments that have resulted in violating black bodies.

What was tragic however was to hear the pain he feels from being caught in the middle of two competing worlds. White officers are constantly looking to see if he is willing to hold members of the community accountable when they break the law, and the black community, in particular, is watching him with an eye of suspicion because he represents an entity that has historically been an agent of terror and violence in our community. When I told him that being consistent in demonstrating that he is part of the black community and wants to help them will pay dividends eventually, he told me that he has been showing love to members of the community on his current beat, speaking to them and affirming their humanity. He told me that the older guys show him no love back, but when he turned to the younger kids on the playground and began to proactively show them love just because, they responded back. Ultimately reimagining policing will take getting more police officers who have a genuine heart to serve, involved, but for some, having their friends and loved ones become police officers is seen as an act of betrayal. Being a black police officer in America is such a distinctive position to hold in this era of reckoning of race in America as it pertains to police brutality. I walked away from my two-hour conversation with "D" with a much broader perspective about the way in which officers are trained, but I still am not convinced that passing countless policing laws, enacting better recruitment efforts to weed out implicit bias, or creating stiffer penalties will by themselves get us to the promised land of a new way of envisioning policing in America.

This then is the conundrum I feel, when I see marginalized communities conceptualize the steps needed to eradicate the chronic use of excessive force in policing. We focus on what police departments need to do, what white people need to do, but too often we fail to see our own part to play in the struggle. Part of it is, we find succor in pointing the fingers at others, while ignoring or devaluing the ones that point to us. There is a certain amount of satisfaction we the oppressed get in telling the oppressor about themselves, a fleeting joy obtained in putting the beneficiaries of white supremacy on blast. I am neither discounting the numerous issues white people and police departments need to contend with before meaningful change can take place, the multiple chapters prior to this conclusion help bolster that claim, but at the same time, I know we, the black community as a whole, have a role to play beyond pointing fingers and telling others what they need to do. God has chosen us, for whatever reason, to participate in our own emancipation from systemic racism, even as we delight in blaming others. When I say participation, I mean something greater than advocating for meaningful legislation, although that is good. I mean something more than forms of protesting for the purpose of demanding police accountability, although I believe them to be a necessary part of the equation. And I endorse the implementation of economic sanctions by the black community that would target our dollars solely into supporting institutions that either proactively empower our community or demonstrate their commitment to ending systemic racism in its various forms. All of those things are needed and more. If we want to truly reimagine policing in America, then we must think holistically.

The Hypocrisy of Demonizing the Police and Appropriating the Language of Violence

When we flush out Girard's analysis of the pervasiveness of violence in our society, those of us in the black community need to have honest conversations about how we love to point out everybody else's violence, but too often we are silent about our own. I was saddened to see Lebron

James prematurely tweet out "you're next," and post a picture of officer Nicholas Reardon who shot and killed Ma'khia Bryant just days after the world witnessed a jury convict Derek Chauvin on multiple murder charges. Saddened not because I believe he was intentionally trying to promote violence, but that he let his anger get the best of him, and had he just waited until he collected his thoughts, settled his emotions, and gathered the facts of the case, he could've stated similar sentiments about accountability with language more difficult for his haters to twist for nefarious reasons. Lovers of violent scapegoating were quick to jump on the demonizing bandwagon, noting how Lebron's platform has the potential to transform tweets into dog whistles that incite violence.

If you think derogatory terms or threatening phrases used to describe police officers are inconsequential, consider Ismaaiyl Brinsley, who in December of 2014, shot his girlfriend, was incensed about the killings of Eric Garner and Michael Brown, drove from Baltimore to Brooklyn, NY, shot and killed Officers Rafael Ramos and Wenjian Liu sitting in their squad car. Those two cops deserve their names to be said just like George Floyd, Sandra Bland, Philando Castile and so many more. He so loved the moniker of calling police pigs, that he claimed on social media, ""I'm Putting Wings On Pigs Today. They Take 1 Of Ours . . . Let's Take 2 of Theirs #ShootThePolice #RIPErivGardner #RIPMikeBrown." This was violent scapegoating on steroids, and it was a perfect window of opportunity for protestors who had violently clashed with officers during marches in various cities to model the words and behaviors that they want the police to model when someone who they revere has been violated, but that didn't happen. For the most part, officers in New York and across the country were left to grieve for themselves, and protestors who demanded the officers affirm their humanity suddenly weren't aggressively fighting for the humanity of those murdered public servants. One of the most prophetic voices in that moment, wasn't from a civil rights icon, wasn't from the church, it was from President Barak Obama, who stated, ". . . Tonight, I ask people to reject violence and words that harm, and turn to words that heal—prayer, patient dialogue, and sympathy for the friends and family of the fallen." This was a perfect opportunity for two sides to come together and heal. But that can't happen when many in the black community are comfortable demonizing police officers indiscriminately in ways that are similar to how they demonize us. Of course, representatives from New York police blamed the protestors who had filled the streets of New York after a grand jury declined to bring criminal charges in the case of Eric Garner, a black Staten Island man who died after a police chokehold. "There's blood on many hands tonight—those that incited violence on the street under the guise of protests, that tried to tear down what New York City police officers did every day," the head of the Patrolmen's Benevolent Association, Patrick Lynch, said outside Woodhull Hospital. Somehow, he skipped over the reason why folks were in the streets protesting in the first place, but regardless, the mudslinging sticks when you provide a rough surface for it to cling to, and because we have strayed so far from the nonviolent tenets of Dr. Martin Luther King Jr., we are left trying to win the debate by saying that the isolated incidents of violence during protests aren't as bad as violence perpetrated by the police. The "my wrong isn't as bad as yours" strategy rarely is compelling, and it is why, after our predecessors scoffed at King's nonviolent stance, our straying from his principles hasn't netted substantial gains to build upon King's success in having the country see who really was on the right side of history. King understood the moral power behind nonviolence and refused to associate in any way with those willing to stoop to the level of the agents of white supremacy.

Not only are leaders who are trying to call out police brutality silent or defensive when it comes to tamping down the violent rhetoric and the destruction of property, but some have also grossly misappropriated the language of King to support the violence. As protestors retaliated against the militarization of police in Ferguson, Missouri, after Mike Brown's death in 2014, some tried to use King's famous words, "a riot is the language of the unheard," to draw empathy, and King's famous phrase was revived last summer as violent destruction of property broke out in Kenosha, Wisconsin; Minneapolis, Minnesota; Seattle, Washington; Portland, Oregon; and New York City just to name a few cities.

On September 27, 1966, King availed himself to be interviewed by CBS chief news correspondent Mike Wallace. The interview begins with establishing where King stood on violence, "I will never change in my basic idea that nonviolence is the most potent weapon available to the Negro in his struggle for freedom and justice. I think for the Negro to turn to violence would be both impractical and immoral." When Mike Wallace presses him on the reality that there are some in the black community who feel differently, King acknowledges their existence, states that they are a minority, then he shifts to hold white America accountable, "I contend that the cry of "black power" is, at bottom, a reaction to the reluctance of white power to make the kind of changes necessary to make justice a reality for the Negro. I think that we've got to see that a riot is the language of the unheard."

In '67, King reiterated his vehement disagreement with violent riots as an effective tool for protest, stating that he believed violent riots helped right-wing extremists like George Wallace. In '68, he doubled down on his stance, even as civil rights groups became all the more frustrated with the persistence of violence upon black and brown bodies. When placed in their proper context, King's language about riots is so far from a ringing endorsement as characterized by some modern-day civil rights advocates. To parse out the famous phrase and not include its proper context of denouncing reactionary violence does a grave disservice to the legacy of one of the greatest protestors we have ever seen.

Not only do we do a grave disservice to King, but we also run counter to the teachings of Jesus, who gave us specific instructions in how to respond to those who use their power to dehumanize and humiliate the weak and the vulnerable. Matthew 5: 38-48 to me is one of the most inciteful, instructive texts that both speak to the dynamics of police brutality and whose insights King incorporated into his principles of nonviolence. On November 17, 1957, at Dexter Baptist Church in Montgomery, Alabama, King preached the sermon "Love Your Enemies," and took Matthew 5: 43-45 as his text. The sermon focuses on answering the question, how do we love our enemies, and King answers the question by stating that, "in order to love your enemies, you must begin by analyzing self… It seems to me that that is the first and foremost way to come to an adequate discovery to the how of this situation… A second thing that an individual must do in seeking to love his enemy is to discover the element of good in his enemy… the person who hates you most has some good in him; even the nation that hates you most has some good in it; even the race that hates you most has some good in it… Another way that you love your enemy is this: When the opportunity presents itself for you to defeat your enemy, that is the time which you must not do it… Love is creative, understanding goodwill for all men. It is the refusal to defeat any individual. When you rise to the level of love, of its great beauty and power, you seek only to defeat evil systems."

While most of King's famous sermon preached at his own church based its insights from Matthew 5: 43-45, there was one small section that took its cue from Matthew 5: 38-41; "There is a power in love that our world has not discovered yet. Jesus discovered it centuries ago. Mahatma Gandhi of India discovered it a few years ago, but most men and most women never discover it. For they believe in hitting for hitting; they believe in an eye for an eye and a tooth for a tooth; they believe in hating for hating; but Jesus comes to us and says, 'This isn't the way.'" Here King champions Jesus' principle of non-retaliation, envisioning it as a powerful tool able to bring down strongholds, but that the world hasn't discovered yet. Dr. Obery Hendricks, in his groundbreaking publication *The Politics of Jesus*, does a masterful job applying his distinctive, guerilla exegesis to this passage. In chapter 4 of his classic publication, Hendricks explains 7 political strategies of Jesus, and the 6th strategy, "Take Blows Without Returning Them," is grounded in this significant scripture. Hendricks sees this passage as Jesus giving a master plan to the vulnerable who are targets on the frontlines of a cosmic war and are being confronted by powerful entities that delight in violating them. Hendricks' breakdown of the Jesus' teaching in the Matthean text aligns with King's theology by recovering the very political, proactive, and powerful nature of nonviolence resistance. Informed by American theologian Walter Wink, Hendricks skillfully rescues from obscurity and shame Jesus' famous instruction of giving our enemies who have struck our right cheek, our left in return. In so doing, God's Word helps us transform from helpless scapegoats succumbing to power, to victorious lambs wielding power through suffering to resist dehumanization. In one fell swoop, *The Politics of Jesus* telegraphs Jesus being a political revolutionary as He empowers the helpless to nonviolently fight back against the Jewish elite and Roman government, both of whom have ritualized violently scapegoating the poor. In this way, when we fully commit to the notion that "turning the other cheek is a powerful act of self-determination," we will realize that this passage is uniquely qualified to show us how to respond to police brutality today. King understood it, but we've strayed from the places our God where we met thee, we have become so drunk with the wine of needing to riot as a result of being violently scapegoated that we have yet to discover the power of turning the other cheek. And I believe it is no stretch to proclaim George Floyd's murder unleashed a power no retaliatory action could muster. Its sheer vileness ushed in a movement that still reverberates today.

If we are bending over backwards to defend riots stemming from the police killing us . . . I ask, what moral standing do we have to forcefully shame the agents of white supremacy who stormed the Capitol on January 6th? To claim that January 6th was infinitely worse because they were attempting to overthrow the peaceful transfer of government by storming, looting and desecrating the most cherished site of our democracy (having actualized the marching orders from then President Trump), in an attempt to push back on drawing false equivalency is both valid and impotent at the same time. Valid because the egregiousness of one far exceeds the other, impotent because it is all violence, they are both feeble attempts to grasp privilege, and neither contribute to ceasing violence against the other, in fact, they justify it. Again Hendricks hits the nail on its head in his seminal work, *The Politics of Jesus*, when he speaks about the shortcomings of liberalism, "without a religious or spiritual referent, in many cases liberal discourse has become self-referential, stressing liberal ideas versus the spirituality that inspired them."

King understood the moral and political leverage gained from "policing" his protests, ensuring that participants were aware and compliant to the principle of nonviolence. He demanded it because it made the audacity of the perpetrators of violence more visible and intolerable to accept. And the suffering endured for being nonviolent gave the movement the moral power needed to sustain a campaign long enough to change history. This is what it means to embody the theology of a lamb. The innocence of the lamb is its means to triumph over violence through nonviolence. This is the mark of authentic servant leadership. It means refusing to grasp at privilege and be willing to sacrifice for the greater good. It is a tough pill for the victims of police brutality to swallow, but righteous indignation cannot be a cover (remember "yipper" in Leviticus 16) to hide our own tendency to demonize and stereotype others. Girard's mimetic desire may be at play here! King's nonviolence stance was a prophetic warning that justice will remain elusive because the movement loses its moral high ground when it uses violence and/or fails to vehemently oppose it. Even the prosecutor Jerry Blackwell understood that the murder of George Floyd, the aftermath, including the verdict convicting Derek Chauvin on all three counts created a "moral moment."

This is exactly why I have even more admiration for Lebron James now than I had prior to April 21, 2021. He realized his initial tweet was a mistake and instead of doubling down on a mistake, instead of making justifications to defend his error, he honored the moral moment by proactively removing the tweet. He apologized and re-countered with a statement that better reflected his desire to see change and combined it with temperance to seek wisdom versus wading in emotionalism. Some will say he had no choice because he put Twitter and the companies he represents and endorses in a tough spot, but I cannot emphasize enough how laudable it is to see a powerful black man not succumb to the trend of the times, which has seen influential people be rewarded by the extreme fringes of their political base, for doubling down on lies. His move not only saved his bag, but it neutralized the neoconservatives who would have had justification to persist in violent language to scapegoat, because his unwillingness to acknowledge his own culpability would've given them cover. Instead, they were left to focus on the initial reaction, and try to minimize the proactive revision, specifically because they want the privilege of not having to revise their own penchant for violence. Words matter, and words of provocation definitely matter, lest we forget we are not that far removed from January 6, when former President Trump and his minions used words of provocation which were appropriated by "protestors" to storm the Capitol and attempt a coup d'état. As I listened to progressive media outlets try to defend Maxine Waters' comments (the day before the verdict to get "more confrontational" if Derek Chauvin was found not guilty) and Lebron James' tweet "you're next," we cannot have it both ways. Whenever you try to criticize someone for doing something, but then want to make justification for you doing essentially the same thing, you've prevented yourself from accessing the leverage needed to gain authority and credibility. As much as we can look to legislators to craft laws and policies that hold police accountable for the use of excessive force, as much as we can demand front line law enforcement agents and passive beneficiaries of systemic racism to expose and tear down the structures in multiple sectors of our society that demonize, criminalize, and violate black and brown people to keep them subjugated under white control, if we remain blind to our own enabling and facilitation of perpetuating violence against each other as well as nonblack individuals, and the police, we are short-circuiting any real possibility at achieving reform and rebuilding a new way of policing.

We want the police to purge themselves of using excessive force, even in sometimes difficult split-second decision-making, but then turn around and want police and everybody else to condone allowing protestors to transition to rioters, destroying property, looting, throwing objects and weaponizing the language of violence when we confront police in the streets. We cannot demand police to affirm our humanity and yet refuse to affirm theirs. We cannot be outraged when police provoke, demonize, criminalize and violate black and brown bodies, but then we are silent or defensive, or cling to some right to use the language of provocation or even outright demonization, "pigs in a blanket, fry 'em like bacon." Not a cell in my body believes Lebron was promoting violence, but can we vouch for the mindset of every single LBJ fan, one of whom may possibly see "you're next" as a call to take out a police officer? That is the problem. "Oh well, it's just words;" and in believing that, we legitimize and minimize the words on the mall in DC that incited the mob on January 6. "But we are on the right side of the argument"; really? It is hard to tell when the language of violence towards the police appropriates the same speech used to characterize police officers being attacked while sitting in their squad cars in Brooklyn, or being ambushed by a sniper who kills five police officers on July 7, 2016, in Dallas Texas, or when a driver rams his car into Capitol Police. Thank you Lebron for admitting your misstep and recalibrating your words to express your outrage with the fatal shooting, while at the same time creating distance between the circumstances of George Floyd's murder and Ma'kia Bryant's killing. Both were undesirable outcomes. But if we don't want white folk to draw false equivalencies in comparing the act of domestic terrorism on January 6th with the riots that sprung up over numerous cities last summer ("there were good people on both sides"), then first, let's recognize the hypocrisy of clinging to violence when we do it and attempting to castigate others when they do it. Furthermore, we lose credibility and moral authority when we become arbiters of false equivalency ourselves, as if all police shootings of black and brown bodies are a gross injustice. The reality is so much more complex; all police use of force exercised against black and brown bodies is not the same. Each circumstance has unique factors which demand that as a community we do not rush to judgment, and when necessary, follow Lebron's wisdom in pulling back to become informed about the facts, instead of prematurely yielding to appeal to our emotions, even as we want the killing to stop.

God's Word Shows Us How Powerful Lambs Are

I Kings 3:16-28: 16 Later, two women who were prostitutes came to the king and stood before him. 17 The one woman said, "Please, my lord, this woman and I live in the same house; and I gave birth while she was in the house. 18 Then on the third day after I gave birth, this woman also gave birth. We were together; there was no one else with us in the house, only the two of us were in the house. 19 Then this woman's son died in the night, because she lay on him. 20 She got up in the middle of the night and took my son from beside me while your servant slept. She laid him at her breast and laid her dead son at my breast. 21 When I rose in the morning to nurse my son, I saw that he was dead; but when I looked at him closely in the morning, clearly it was not the son I had borne." 22 But the other woman said, "No, the living son is mine, and the dead son is yours." The first said, "No, the dead son is yours, and the living son is mine." So they argued before the king. 23 Then the king said, "The one says, 'This is my son that is alive, and your son is dead'; while the other says, 'Not so! Your son is dead, and my son is the living one.'" 24 So the king said, "Bring me a sword," and they brought a sword before the king. 25 The king said, "Divide the living boy in two; then give half to the one, and half to the other." 26 But the woman whose son was alive said to the king—because compassion for her son burned within her—"Please, my lord, give her the living boy; certainly do not kill him!" The other said, "It shall be neither mine nor yours; divide it." 27 Then the king responded: "Give the first woman the living boy; do not kill him. She is his mother." 28 All Israel heard of the judgment that the king had rendered; and they stood in awe of the king, because they perceived that the wisdom of God was in him, to execute justice.

In the beginning, one could easily state that these two women were equivalent, when it is clear by the end of the narrative, they are worlds apart. The writer of 1 Kings deliberately delivers the narration to help us see how much alike they are initially, noting their shared occupation, that they lived in the same house, and that each had a son, born days apart. From there, however, the differences slowly emerge. One mother inadvertently killed her son, laying on him while sleeping, and switches her dead son with the alive son while the other mother is sleeping. The next morning, the other mother notices the switch, and an argument ensues, which cannot be settled without a ruling from the king. When making their case to the king, notice initially how the language of the two mothers is so similar that the king cannot differentiate who is right and who is wrong. It is only when the king threatens to exert violence on the innocent that the contrast between the two mothers is readily apparent. As the king was ready to divide the alive son in half, one mother said —"Please, my lord, give her the living boy; certainly do not kill him," while the other mother said, "It shall be neither mine nor yours; divide it." One was willing to sacrifice her own to prevent the continuation of violence, because *compassion burned within her*, while the other was willing to allow the violence to continue. Even though we know that police brutality is not about a bad apple here or there but about a system born from a white supremacist heritage, the question God's Word has for us is this: is compassion burning within us that we are willing to sacrifice to stop the violence, or are we so hell-bent on calling out our oppressors that we lose sight of the larger objective? As I have preached before in sermons, we have earned PhDs in the art of scrutinizing the specks in everybody else's eyes, but all of us flunk miserably in removing the log in our own. The ability for us to separate ourselves from those trying to create false equivalency is accessed through sacrifice, re-embracing King's commitment to nonviolent protests, owning our own mimetic desire to cling to privilege, and doing our part in our own contexts as well as our dealings with others to prevent the persistence of violence. The text tells us that the woman whose son was alive was willing to protect it from violence even if it meant losing her son to a scapegoater. It was more important for the real mother of the child to cease the violence than win the battle of words and image. The wise king was able to clearly draw distinction between the two and rewarded the true mother of the baby. This is the essence of how a lamb is triumphant. Instead, we have allowed the onslaught of violent scapegoating from our oppressor to trick us into believing that we don't need to combat the violence we perpetuate, which eviscerates any moral or political leverage we would obtain. As former First Lady Michelle Obama said, "when they do low, we go high!"

I'm Starting with The Man in the Mirror

This book has focused on the scapegoat mechanism being alive and well as a sacred tool and tactic of police officers operating under implicit racial bias, who have ritualized the use of excessive force to brutalize black and brown bodies. I am tempted to go over implicit bias and systemic racism in all of its iterations in our criminal justice system and uncover the diverse, systemic ways in which the scapegoat mechanism operates. From how federal prosecutors are more likely to charge black and brown people with offenses that carry harsh mandatory minimum sentences, to police misconduct that may not necessarily involve the use of physical force, to the ways in which district attorneys and grand juries scapegoat, to the legacy of judges at the local, state, and federal level imposing longer sentences to black defendants versus their white counterparts, I am quite confident that a thorough investigation into each of these sectors, would uncover the scapegoat mechanism at work. Such uncovering is well beyond the scope of this present work, but it is scholarship that I believe needs to be done, taking its cues from the classic work of Michelle Alexander in *The New Jim Crow*, and it would be of benefit to humanity in strengthening the argument that scapegoating is not just a tool of police officers, it is pervasive throughout our criminal justice system.

In addition to those elements, what I believe is missing is for us as members of the black community to own our role in facilitating the ritual of violence so prevalent in our culture. During the April 27, 2021 press conference held by the family of Andrew Brown Jr., who had been killed by a North Carolina police officer just days before, some protestors were yelling from the back of the crowd about transitioning from peaceful protesting to violent retribution. Khalil Ferebee, who had painfully watched his father being killed, got on the mic and stated, "it's too much violence going on . . . with blacks killing each other . . . violence is not the key." For a young black man who was still in pain about watching his father die at the hands of violence, to resist retaliation and challenge the community to find a nonviolent way to confront this ongoing crisis was heartwarming. It is our calling to find a multitude of ways to shame, to aggressively confront the perpetrators who hide behind shield and ritual to commit acts of violence, to hold police officers accountable for the disparity between how blacks are treated versus white people, and yes, Dr. West, to even commit acts of defiance to send the message that violent scapegoating will not be allowed to persist unchecked. The God we serve empowers us to see death for a righteous cause not as defeat but as victory. The cause is worth dying for, but at the end of the day, you all need to stop killing us. Our job is to mine the scriptures to help us discern how to confront dehumanization in its various contexts, create a culture of self-love and self-defense that conveys the message that when you scapegoat us, God positions us to become victorious lambs able to pull down strongholds otherwise impossible to defeat.

As much as I believe that the work of investigating scapegoating in America's criminal justice system is necessary, scapegoating is not just a tool exclusively institutionalized in our criminal justice system for the purpose of keeping black and brown people under control; scapegoating is alive and kicking outside of criminal justice. In our financial system, our labor system, our healthcare system, our educational system, our political system, and even in our faith institutions, scapegoating unquestionably exists. When we consider Rene Girard's assertion that scapegoating is a phenomenon of pandemic proportions, it needs to be teased out in its diverse iterations across the world. Scapegoating is not just situated in our criminal justice system, it is infused throughout our culture comprehensively, it is not exclusively an American notion, it is global in terms of its impact, and it doesn't just exist within issues surrounding race, it flourishes within the power relationship dynamics within gender, sexual orientation, religion, and class, just to name a few.

We must begin to see the dehumanization of black and brown bodies in the form of police brutality as part of a much larger system well outside the boundaries of policing and even law enforcement. The addiction to violence against communities of color in policing is tied to the larger agendas of scapegoating grounded in white fear and white greed endemic in our culture. In other words, we are fooling ourselves in terms of ending the powerful effects of police brutality in policing unless we appreciate how racism functions through a multitude of coordinated social-political systems designed to keep masses of black and brown people disconnected from achieving the American dream outside white control. Racism's addiction to violent scapegoating in the form of police brutality is so infused in the very DNA of America, that complete detoxification from it in law enforcement will truly be possible when we are serious about eradicating the vestiges of white supremacy across the board. Trying to reimagine policing separate and disconnected from reimagining community is an exercise in futility.

If Rene Girard is correct about the pervasiveness of violence and scapegoating in the very fabric of our culture, in our collective psyche, then marginalized communities must also self-reflect and begin to see how we contribute to the dysfunction of society when we normalize scapegoating in our own contexts. There are many types of relationships where mimetic desire is stoked by fears and threats that lead to scapegoating and I believe God has called even those who have been chronically scapegoated to see ways in which we enable scapegoating to persist. Some may be tempted to believe that I am putting the weight of the responsibility to carry the burden of fighting for justice on the scapegoated but let me assure you that victim-blaming is not my aim or goal. When Jesus tells the scapegoated to love their enemies, turn the other cheek, and shun retaliation, his challenge to those victimized is not about blaming them. My framework in terms of seeing and challenging members from every demographic to look within to purge the language and culture of nefarious scapegoating from various sources is rooted in the belief that police brutality will never be eliminated until we are serious about owning and confronting the insidious ways in which scapegoating operates in numerous contexts and is not just perpetuated externally upon us, but also internally from within us.

Furthermore, I know that as a black man, I need to follow the example of Lebron James and own my own tendencies to scapegoat in certain situations. There are times when I have appropriated violent rhetoric in righteous indignation or when my emotions get the best of me. This work is a challenge for me to deal with my own character flaws across the board. The members of Family of Faith A.M.E. Church know that when I preach, I am not preaching at them; but instead, God's message is a challenge for all of us in the room, especially me. I am intentionally leaning into this moment because God gave me the word scapegoat after witnessing George Floyd's murder. From that one word, a sermon was created, and by the end of the sermon, God had me write out the chapters for this book in about 9 minutes and 29 seconds (give or take)! I hope this book provides fresh perspectives on a persistent, pernicious problem. I would love to create a body of work that showcases how engaging creatively with God's Word informs and encourages us to find agency in confronting systemic problems and impact our world. ServantLeaderMinistries.com is not only a website where this book will be sold, it will be the virtual repository of resources to help communities use biblical principles baked in "hood exegesis" to bring down strongholds in our societies.

Conclusion

I applaud the efforts of those who see legislation as a key to silencing police brutality. I worked on Capitol Hill in the US House and Senate when the Affordable Care Act was passed, and currently do research for the Senator-at-Large here in the U.S. Virgin Islands, Steven D. Payne, Sr. But having now appreciated the realization that police brutality historically functions as sacred ritual, we must recognize that legislation alone is not the answer. George Floyd was lynched/crucified, and praise God, a young girl embraced nonviolent resistance (lamb theology) and caught it on video. Gruesome yes, unprecedented no. Why did it in this instance blow a hole in the invincible blue wall, when other murders did not? As a follower of Jesus, the only thing that makes sense to me, is that the war we are fighting is not merely physical, it is spiritual. As Dr. Cornel West told me after one of his classes at Princeton University, humans cannot start movements alone. Something got a hold of Chauvin when he encountered Floyd. Was the violent confrontation influenced by their prior relationship, both having worked in security for a nearby establishment? We may never know. But whatever spirit got a hold of Chauvin in that encounter, helped create an opening in the blue wall such that police officers across the country condemned Chauvin's actions. An unprecedented action long overdue that doesn't solve anything, but undeniably bends the universe toward the arc of justice. God's Word is uniquely qualified to help us reverse engineer police brutality not only because it is both theology (study of God) and anthropology (study of man) rolled into one, but also because it tells us that "we wrestle not against flesh and blood, but against principalities and the rulers of darkness. Against spiritual wickedness in high places" (Ephesians 6:12 KJV). Furthermore, when we resist the trap of the lure of retaliatory violence we position ourselves to love and affirm humanity while defeating evil and the demonic spirits working behind the scenes: "the weapons of our warfare are not carnal, but mighty through God to the pulling down of strongholds" (2 Corinthians 10:4).

At the end of the day, are we really serious about working to end violent scapegoating in the form of police brutality, or do we want to delight in pointing our fingers at others, while refusing to look in the mirror and see how our own penchant for violence undermines our moral authority and credibility to demand the police stop being violent? In order for us to have a real chance of obtaining true justice and righteousness that reimagines police departments eradicating the use of excessive force, we have to wrestle valiantly with God's sacred text and uncover divine strategies to fight on multiple levels. We must see the violence of the police who scapegoat as a function of sacred ritual passed down from generation to generation, and taking cues from Dr. King, we must build a diverse coalition willing to embody the innocence of a lamb, identifying and rooting out various ways violence functions as sacred ritual beyond police brutality. This fight requires remaining steadfastly pure in intention, unyielding to the temptation to lower our standards for political expediency or to enrich our individual capitalistic agendas and when we do so, we can expose the ungodliness of the scapegoaters so that the record is clear and there is no doubt about who is right and who is wrong. I fully support the fight for laws to create accountability for the perpetrators and enablers of police brutality, but we must also wage this war on multiple fronts. It is not an "either/or," but a "both/and" proposition.

NOTES

Introduction

xvi **excessive force** See https://www.youtube.com/watch?v=WEJ9GSzaXTU.

Chapter 1: The More Things Change, the More They Stay the Same

2 **be achieved** See Eric Charles White, *Kaironomia: On the Will to Invent,* 1987, pg. 13.

3 **told CNBC** See https://www.cnbc.com/2020/06/08/police-brutality-protests-pop-up-in-small-towns-in-trump-country.html.

4 **the statement continued** See https://www.france24.com/en/20200613-after-the-death-of-george-floyd-africa-mobilises-against-police-violence.

4 **she said** See https://edition.cnn.com/2020/06/01/world/george-floyd-global-protests-intl/index.html.

4 **he stated** https://www.cnbc.com/2020/05/29/former-officer-involved-in-death-of-george-floyd-has-been-arrested.html.

5 **benefit of hindsight** See https://www.washingtonpost.com/news/morning-mix/wp/2014/12/04/why-its-so-difficult-to-charge-police-officers-who-kill/.

5 **in his ruling** See https://edition.cnn.com/2020/11/05/us/george-floyd-officers-trial/index.html.

5 **violence and crime** See https://www.brookings.edu/blog/fixgov/2020/06/19/ what-does-defund-the-police-mean-and-does-it-have-merit/.

6 **stop happening** See https://www.bostonglobe.com/2020/06/04/nation/ayanna-pressley-justin-amash-introduce-bill-end-prohibition-lawsuits-against-police-officers/.

6 **police investigations** See https://judiciary.house.gov/uploadedfiles/fact sheet justice in policing_act_of_2020.pdf?utm_campaign=2927-519.

6 **Tally Clerk** See https://www.rawstory.com/3-republicans-accused-ethics-violation/ Sarah K. Burris March 4, 2021.

7 **its flag** See https://indianexpress.com/article/explained/explained-why-the-us-state-of-mississippi-got-a-new-flag-6946928/.

7 **police officers** See https://americanpoliceofficersalliance.com/defund-the-police-these-cities-said-yes/.

7 **spoke volumes** See https://www.independent.co.uk/news/world/americas/ trump-minneapolis-protest-looting-shooting-twitter-quote-police-a9538996.html.

9 **Covid-19 lockdown** See https://www.france24.com/en/20200613-after-the-death-of-george-floyd-africa-mobilises-against-police-violence.

9 **of Covid-19** Ibid.

14 **in 1838** See "The Long Painful History of Police Brutality in the US," Katie Nodjimbadem, SMITHSONIANMAG.COM, JULY 27, 2017.

14 **police killings** Ibid.

15 **by eternity** See Georges Tavard *Paul Tillich and the Christian Message*. New York: Scribner, 1962 pg.88-89.

Chapter 2: Leviticus 16 Responds to Violent Scapegoating in Genesis 37

17 **their holiness** See Stephen M. Miller, *The Complete Guide to the Bible*, 2007.

18 **their sins** See *The New Interpreter's Bible Commentary*, "The Book of Leviticus" by Walter C. Kaiser Jr. pg. 986.

18 **sacrificial system** Ibid. pg. 987-88.

19 **the people** Ibid. pg. 1109.

21 **Mesopotamian Literature** See "The Disposal of Impurity: Elimination Rites in the Bible and in Hittite and Mesopotamian Literature," SBLDS 101 (Atlanta, GA, 1987), by D.P. Wright.

21 **complicated history** See Calum Carmichael, "The Origin of the Scapegoat Ritual," *Vestus Testamentum*, Apr. 2000, Vol. 50, Fasc. 2, pg. 167.

21 **Genesis 37** See Ibid pp. 167-182 and Howard Cooper, "Some Thoughts on 'Scapegoating' and Its Origins in Leviticus 16," *European Judaism: A journal for the New Europe*, Autumn 2008, pp. 112-119.

22 **Book of Jubilees 34, 18** See Ibid. pg. 170.

22 **the scapegoat** Ibid. pg. 174.

23 **brother's keeper** See Cooper, pg. 115.

24 **Day of Atonement** See Carmichael, pg. 171 and Jacob Milgrom, *Leviticus 1-16*, pg. 257.

26 **good news** See Terence F. Fretheim, *New Interpreters Bible Commentary* on Genesis.

26 **him headache** See Rochel Chein, https://www.chabad.org/parshah/article_cdo/ aid/1736781/jewish/Did-Jacob-Ever-Discover-What-the-Brothers-Did-to-Joseph.htm.

27 **their behalf** Ibid.

30 **strengths and weaknesses** See Chandler Collins, "Kipper and the Yom Kippur Rituals in the Discourse of Leviticus 16," Master's Thesis Project, Moody Bible Institute, 2008.

31 **Hebrew Bible** Ibid. pg. 3.

31 **identical word** See Ludwig Köhler and Walter Baumgartner, *The Hebrew and Aramaic Lexicon of the Old Testament*, 2 vols. (Boston: Brill, 2001) pg. 494.

31 **those cases** See Richard Averbeck, "כפר" *in New International Dictionary of Old Testament Theology and Exegesis,* ed. Willem VanGemeren, vol. 2 (Grand Rapids: Zondervan, 1997) [689–710] pp. 692-693.

31 **Yitzhaq Feder** See Yitzhaq Feder, "Blood Expiation in Hittite and Biblical Ritual," (Atlanta: *Society of Biblical Literature*, 2011) pg. 168.

31 **in scripture** See Collins, pg. 8.

32 **to purge** Ibid., pg. 8.

32 **appeasement/ransom** See Nobuyoshi Kiuchi, *Leviticus* (Downers Grove: InterVarsity, 2007) pp. 56-57.

32 **same way** See Collins, pp. 10-11.

32 **Hebrew Bible** Ibid. pg. 20.

34 **his commentary** Ibid. pg. 23.

34 **ritual impurities** Roy Gane, *Cult and Character* (Winona Lake, IN: Eisenbrauns, 2005).

35 **ritual altogether** See Collins, pg. 56.

35 **Milgrom do** Ibid., pg. 76.

36 **goal depended** Ibid., pg. 80.

38 **the Bible** https://sydneyjewishmuseum.com.au/jewish-culture/the-origins-of-the-scapegoat/.

38 **Temple Judaism** "The Scapegoat Tradition: A Study in Early Jewish Interpretation" by Lester L. Grabbe, pg. 158.

38 **proper name** Collins, pg. 45.

38 **healing of the land** Grabbe pg. 156.

38 **children of Israel** Roger De Verteuil, *Journal of Religion & Health.* July 1966. Vol.5, No. 3, pg. 213.

39 **to go away** Carmichael, pg. 178.

Chapter 3: Reenvisioning Isaiah 53: Reinterpreting the Voices, Navigating the Theological Shift from Scapegoats to Lambs

41 **Christ's suffering** Joy Freemyer's "Four Interpretations of Isaiah 53: An Historical Excursus," a 2013 thesis for the Honors College at Baylor University.

41 **prior legacy** Christopher R. Seitz *The New Interpreters Bible Commentary* on Isaiah 40-66, Abingdon Press, 2001, pg. 460.

41 **left off** Seitz, pg. 476.

41 **the nations** Ibid., pg. 461.

42 **servant's destiny** Ibid., pg. 462.

42 **recognition of the nations** Ibid., pg. 463.

43 **and the kings** Michael L. Barre,"Textual and Rhetorical-critical Observations on the Last Servant Song (Isaiah 52:13-53:12)," January 2000, *The Catholic Biblical Quarterly*, pg. 9.

43 **the Servant** Barre, pg. 11.

43 **hand of the Lord** Seitz, pg. 465.

44 **of the Servant** Barre, pg. 12.

44 **to the nations** Seitz pg. 465.

44 **let alone violence** Barre, pg. 13.

44 **accruing to others** Seitz, pg. 466.

45 **human agency** Barre, pg. 15.

45 **he delights** John Gill's Exposition of the Entire Bible. https://www.studylight.org/commentaries/eng/geb/isaiah-53.html.

46 **a death** Seitz,. pg. 466.

46 **from God** Barre, pg. 20.21.

Chapter 4: Revelations from the Function of Scapegoating in the Gospel Narratives

50 **and dying** *The Complete Guide to the Bible*, pp.318.

53 breadth **of God's love** *The New Interpreter's Bible Commentary*, pg. 108.

55 **likelihood poor** M. Eugene Boring, *The New Interpreters Bible Commentary*, pg. 278).

55 **mistreatment of others** Obery Hendricks *The Politics of Jesus* pg. 162.

56 **Mark 2:9** Gail R. O'Day, *The New Interpreter's Bible Commentary*, pg. 578.

56 **and walk** Ibid., pg. 579.

57 **in the world** Ibid., pg. 581.

59 **each other** Pheme Hawkins, *The New Interpreter's Bible*, pg. 563.

62 **him imprisoned** Rene Girard, *The Scapegoat*, Johns Hopkins University Press, 1986, pg. 169.

63 **1 Kings 17-19** M. Boring, *The New Interpreter's Bible Commentary*, pg. 319.

64 **Antipas versus Salome** Rene Girard, The Scapegoat pg. 129.

68 **correctional control** https://www.aclu.org/feature/police-practices.

69 **before testimony** Boring, *The New Interpreter's Bible*, pg. 480.

69 **get rid of Jesus** R. Allen Culpepper, The New Interpreter's Bible, pg. 414.

69 **Greek curative exit ritual** Jennifer K. Berenson Maclean, "Barabbas, the Scapegoat Ritual, and the Development of the Passion Narrative," published in the *Harvard Theological Review*, 2007, pg. 312.

70 **rest of the Sanhedrin** Raymond Brown, *Death of a Messiah*, Doubleday Publishing, 1994, pg. 172.

72 **words of Pilate** See Raymond Brown's *Death of a Messiah*, and Jennifer K. Berenson Maclean's, "Barabbas, the Scapegoat Ritual, and the Development of the Passion Narrative."

72 **portrayal of him** Gail R. O'Day, New Interpreter's Bible Commentary on the Gospel of John, pg. 815.

73 **Roman culpability** Boring, New Interpreter's Bible Commentary, pg. 486.

73 **one community** Jan Bremmer, "Scapegoat Rituals in Ancient Greece," *Oxford Readings in Greek Religion,* pg. 287.

73 **treated similarly** Jennifer K. Berenson Maclean pg. 314.

73 **Leviticus 16** Ibid., pg. 313.

74 **watch yes** Ibid., pg. 316.

76 **the object** Girard, *Scapegoat*, pg. 117.

Chapter 5: George Floyd the Scapegoat/Lamb in Genesis/Leviticus, Isaiah, and the Gospels

78 **violence upon the scapegoat** Girard. *The Scapegoat*, pg. 142.

79 **counties in 1702** Philip L. Reichel (1992) The Misplaced Emphasis on Urbanization in Police Development," *Policing and Society*, 3:1, 1-12, DOI: 10.1080/10439463.1992.9964653.

79 **the political system** https://plsonline.eku.edu/insidelook/history-policing-united-states-part-1.

80 **Leviticus 16** John Walton, "Azazel and the Scapegoat," March 6, 2009, https://zondervanacademic.com/blog/azazel-and-the-scapegoat.

81 **Joseph's brothers** Carmichael, Calum, "The Origin of the Scapegoat Ritual," *Vestus Testamentum*, Apr. 2000, Vol. 50, Fasc. 2, pg. 167.

82 **justice system** Gene M. Tucker, *New Interpreters Commentary*, pg. 468,

82 **before given** Ibid., pg. 470.

85 **to Bethlehem** https://www.thebiblejourney.org/the-bible-journey/3-jesuss-childhood-journeys-b/the-holy-family-flee-to-egypt/.

89 **out of their mind** Excerpt from the Sermon "When Life Drives Us Out of Our Minds" Part 2, preached by Rev. Charles L. Brown Jr., on October 18, 2020 at Family of Faith A.M.E. Church, St. Thomas, USVI.

89 **to the suffering** Michelle Alexander *The New Jim Crow*, The New Press Publishing, pg. 223.

91 **in the tombs** Excerpt from the Sermon "When Life Drives Us Out of Our Minds" Part 2, preached by Rev. Charles L. Brown Jr., on October 18, 2020 at Family of Faith A.M.E. Church, St. Thomas, USVI.

91 **home and friends** Pheme Perkins, *New Interpreters Commentary* pg. 585.

91 **and rebuilding** https://www.nytimes.com/2020/06/27/us/minneapolis-police-officer-kueng.html.

92 **greatly discouraged** https://www.nytimes.com/2020/06/27/us/minneapolis-police-officer-kueng.html.

92 **and safety** https://isaiahmn.org/2020/05/28/minneapolis-police-department-has-broken-its-oath/.

94 **what's happening** Donald Trump speech, national convention Veterans of Foreign Wars, Tuesday July 24, 2018, Kansas City, Mo.

97 **ritualized extermination** Fleming Rutledge, *The Crucifixion: Understanding the Death of Jesus Christ*, Eerdmans Publishing, 2015, pg. 92.

97 **bestial one** *Southern Horrors: Lynch Law in All Its Phases* by Ida B. Wells (1892).

97 **suspicious activity** https://newsone.com/3049413/police-killings-picked-up-where-lynching-left-off/.

100 **Jesus on the cross** Michael Eric Dyson, *Long Time Coming*, pg. 81, and John Thomas III, https://www.thechristianrecorder.com/the-seven-last-words-of-george-floyd/.

Chapter 6: A Tribute to Rene Girard: The Discoverer of the Scapegoat Mechanism

102 **to Christianity** https://iep.utm.edu/girard/#H1.

104 **sacrificial crisis** https://www.goodreads.com/book/show/337521. Violence and the Sacred.

104 **urban America** https://www.killology.com/publications.

105 **and prohibitions** https://www.enotes.com/topics/violence-sacred.

106 **deadly reciprocity** https://www.goodreads.com/book/show/337521. Violence and the Sacred.

106 **cycle of violence** https://www.enotes.com/topics/violence-sacred/themes.

107 **as scapegoats** https://www.enotes.com/topics/scapegoat-rene-girard/in-depth.

107 **violence itself** "The Scapegoat - Form and Content" *Literary Essentials: Nonfiction Masterpieces* Ed. Frank N. Magill. eNotes.com, Inc. 1989 eNotes.com 5 May, 2021 https://www.enotes.com/topics/scapegoat-rene-girard/in-depth#in-depth-form-and-content.

107 **social peace** https://iep.utm.edu/girard/#SH2d.

108 **compassion for the victim** https://iep.utm.edu/girard/#SH2d.

109 **foundations of culture** https://iep.utm.edu/girard/#SH2d.

109 **Girard is hopeful** "The Scapegoat" *Literary Masterpieces, Volume 9* Ed. Frank Northen Magill. eNotes.com, Inc. 1987 eNotes.com 6 May, 2021 https://www.enotes.com/topics/scapegoat-rene-girard/in-depth#in-depth-scapegoat-1.

110 **into the sky** https://www.pbs.org/wgbh/americanexperience/features/klansville-faq/.

110 **the broader public** https://www.pbs.org/wgbh/americanexperience/features/klansville-faq/.

111 **enforcement personnel** https://timeline.com/white-supremacist-cops-fbi-b28b3b171d56.

112 **social peace** https://iep.utm.edu/girard/.

112 **human violence** "The Scapegoat - Analysis" *Literary Essentials: Nonfiction Masterpieces* Ed. Frank N. Magill. eNotes.com, Inc. 1989 eNotes.com 6 May, 2021 https://www.enotes.com/topics/scapegoat-rene-girard#critical-essays-analysis.

Chapter 7: Where Do We Go from Here?

113 **ultimately are free** Dyson, *Long Time Coming*, pg. 6.

113 **lose your democracy** https://www.youtube.com/watch?v=BWs3sONh_Q&list=PL_Kuv60ypaqwpzzGBNHxHBVzvRrDmxv1&index=11&t=247s.

114 **Police Interaction** https://www.washingtonpost.com/politics/2021/04/20/how-first-statement-minneapolis-police-made-george-floyds-murder-seem-like-george-floyds-fault/.

119 **policing in America** Esau McCaulley, *Reading While Black: African American Biblical Interpretation As An Exercise in Hope.* InterVarsity Press, 2020, pp. 45-46.

120 **are the law** https://timeline.com/white-supremacist-cops-fbi-b28b3b171d56.

120 **white supremacist causes** https://timeline.com/white-supremacist-cops-fbi-b28b3b171d56.

121 **program on extremism** https://www.theguardian.com/us-news/2021/mar/10/fbi-white-supremacists-police-ties-congress https://www.wusa9.com/article/news/national/military-news/the-military-says-some-active-duty-service-members-stormed-the-capitol-now-what-are-they-going-to-do-about-it/65-7ffa2f7c-2ff3-49ca-a7d1-ecb484cc07fe.

123 **across the nation** https://edition.cnn.com/2021/04/14/us/buffalo-officer-reinstated-trnd/index.html.

126 **#RIPMikeBrown** https://www.nytimes.com/2014/12/21/nyregion/two-police-officers-shot-in-their-patrol-car-in-brooklyn.html.

126 **family of the fallen** https://www.nytimes.com/2014/12/21/nyregion/two-police-officers-shot-in-their-patrol-car-in-brooklyn.html.

127 **language of the unheard** https://www.youtube.com/watch?v=_K0BWXjJv5s&list=PL_Kuv60ypaqwpzzGBN-HxHBVzvRrDmxv1&index=17&t=22s.

129 **defeat evil systems** Excerpt from Dr. Martin Luther King Jr's sermon "Love Your Enemies," given at Dexter Baptist Church, Montgomery Alabama, November 17, 1957.

129 **this isn't the way** Ibid.

129 **act of self-determination** Obery Hendricks, *The Politics of Jesus*, pg. 170.

130 **spirituality that inspired them** Ibid., pg. 313.

135 **criminal justice system** Michelle Alexander *The New Jim Crow*, The New Press Publishing, pg. 223.

135 **violence is not the key** https://www.youtube.com/watch?v=VR5XONMSrnI.